THE REMINISCENCES OF
Mr. James E. Hair
Member of the Golden Thirteen

INTERVIEWED BY
Paul Stillwell

U.S. Naval Institute • Annapolis, Maryland

Copyright © 2011

Preface

For the first century and a half of the U.S. Navy's existence, all of its officers were white. It was a situation that was long overdue for correction. In 1943, Adlai E. Stevenson was an assistant to Secretary of the Navy Frank Knox. In a memo, he wrote about the tens of thousands of black sailors then serving the nation during wartime. In the face of mounting political pressure to deal with an obvious shortcoming, the Navy needed to find a remedy for a situation that looked bad and was bad. He proposed to Secretary Knox that the Navy establish a special course to train and commission its first black officers.

From those tens of thousands of young men, the Navy conducted a thorough screening process and selected 16 sailors who had demonstrated records of excellence, particularly in leadership qualities. James Hair was one of the 16 who assembled at Great Lakes, Illinois, in January 1944 to go through a hurry-up training program. Even though all 16 passed the course, only 13 became officers. Hair was one of those commissioned as an ensign. Though they were still treated as second-class citizens even after being commissioned, these men were truly pioneers in the profession. As the years passed and the Navy became much more proactive in seeking diversity in its ranks, Hair and his cohorts retroactively became heroes—known as the Golden Thirteen. They were role models who served as a source of inspiration for later generations of African American naval officers.

In 1986, on behalf of the Naval Institute, I began an oral history project that involved interviewing the eight men who were still alive of the original 13. I recall with mixed emotions visiting Mr. Hair in Hollis, New York, a section of the borough of Queens. His pride in the group's achievement was obvious; the New York State license plate on his car said, "GOLDEN13." The emotions were mixed, though, because not all of his memories were happy ones. He had grown up in Fort Pierce, Florida, at a time when black citizens were routinely mistreated. In the course of one interview, he described the time in 1935 when Estes Wright, the husband of Hair's sister, was lynched. For a time, Hair sobbed and was literally speechless because the memory of that experience was so painful that words would not come. On the other hand, he also described his first reunion with fellow members of the Golden 13—at sea on board the modern destroyer *Kidd*. His fellow pioneers greeted him with joy, for they had not seen him in nearly 40 years. I did a follow-up interview with him in 1988.

Sadly, there are few surviving documentary records of the achievements of the Golden Thirteen. Thus, it was largely through the medium of oral history that their experiences have been preserved. As Christmas of 1991 approached, I arranged to visit Mr. Hair to deliver to him the transcript of our second interview so he could make his inputs. When I arrived at his house, I found a note on the door, written by a neighbor. He said that Hair had been experiencing heart problems and had been taken that morning to the hospital. Mr. Hair died not long after that. As a result, he was not able to be present at Great Lakes, Illinois, in March 1994 when members of the group were feted on the 50th anniversary of their groundbreaking achievement.

In the meantime, in 1993, the Naval Institute published a book I had put together on the Golden Thirteen from interviews with Mr. Hair, seven of his black cohorts, and three white officers who served with them. Among the three was Commander Norman Meyer, who in 1945 had been so impressed by Hair's performance as commanding officer of a tugboat that he invited him to join the crew of the destroyer escort *Mason*.

After the book was published, I received a call from Clarence Wright, who lived in Florida. He told me he was the son of Estes Wright and that he had learned things he had never known from reading the book. He said, "Our mother never told us how our dad had died. She was a good Christian woman, and she didn't want us to grow up hating white people." Some moments truly touch the heart; for me that was one of them.

Prior to his passing, Mr. Hair provided inputs in response to the transcript of the first interview. With both interviews I have done some light editing in the interests of clarity and smoothness. Also, I have inserted footnotes and an index to provide additional information. Janis Jorgensen of the Naval Institute staff has been a friend of long-standing. It was she who coordinated the printing and binding of the finished history.

In completing this volume, the Naval Institute expresses its gratitude to the Tawani Foundation and the Pritzker Military Library of Chicago for their generous financial support of the oral history program that produced this memoir.

Paul Stillwell
U.S. Naval Institute
April 2011

MR. JAMES EDWARD HAIR
MEMBER OF THE GOLDEN THIRTEEN

James Edward Hair was born in Blackville, South Carolina, on 5 August 1915. He grew up in Blackville and later in Fort Pierce, Florida, where his high school was Lincoln Park Academy. He graduated in 1938 from the two-year Bethune-Cookman College in Daytona Beach, Florida; he was the class president. In 1942 he graduated from Xavier University, New Orleans, Louisiana, with a bachelor's degree.

Mr. Hair enlisted in the Navy in 1942 and attended recruit training and quartermaster school at the Great Lakes Naval Training Station, Great Lakes, Illinois. In 1943 he was a quartermaster in the crew of the yard tugboat *Penobscot* (YT-42), which operated from a base in New York City. From January to March 1944, back at Great Lakes, Mr. Hair and 15 other black enlisted men successfully went through a special officer-training course, the first for African Americans in the U.S. Navy. Twelve of the men, including Mr. Hair, were commissioned as ensigns on 17 March 1944; one other member of the group became a warrant officer. Collectively, they subsequently became known as the Golden Thirteen.

As an officer, in 1944-45 Mr. Hair commanded the yard tug *YTB-215*, based in New York City. In May 1945 he reported to the destroyer escort *Mason* (DE-529), a ship with a black enlisted crew and, until Mr. Hair reported, all white officers. He served as the ship's first lieutenant until she was decommissioned later in 1945, following the end of World War II. In 1946 he was first lieutenant on board the tank landing ship *LST-1026* until he received an honorable discharge from the service.

After leaving the service, Mr. Hair worked for a time before taking postgraduate education in social work at Fordham University, New York City. He earned a master's degree in 1950 and then was employed in the social work field for 31 years, including a brief time in Detroit and a much longer period in New York City. He specialized in adoptions and foster care on behalf of the Roman Catholic Church and private agencies.

Mr. Hair died of heart disease on 3 January 1992 at St. Luke's-Roosevelt Hospital in Manhattan. He was survived by daughters Danita Brown and Janette Dent and son James Hair Jr.

Authorization

The U.S. Naval Institute is hereby authorized to make available to individuals, libraries, and other repositories of its choosing the tapes and/or transcripts of two oral history interviews concerning the life and naval career of the late James E. Hair, Sr. The Naval Institute may also, at its discretion, use the material in electronic/digital format, including posting on the Internet. The interviews were recorded on 12 November 1986 and 10 November 1988 in collaboration with Paul Stillwell for the U.S. Naval Institute.

The undersigned, on behalf of the interviewee and other members of the interviewee's family, agrees that the copyright and title to these interviews shall be held jointly by the Hair family and the U.S. Naval Institute. Both the Hair family and the U.S. Naval Institute are entitled to use material as they see fit. The tape recordings of the interviews will remain the property of the U.S. Naval Institute.

Signed and sealed this ___19___ day of ___May___ 2008.

James E. Hair, Jr.

Interview Number 1 with Mr. James E. Hair, member of the Golden Thirteen

Place: Mr. Hair's home in Hollis, New York

Date: Wednesday, 12 November 1986

Paul Stillwell: Mr. Hair, it's a real pleasure to be here and visit with you, to continue in a series I've been doing with various members of the Golden Thirteen. As with them, please start at the very beginning, with your childhood, something about your parents, and your earliest memories.

Mr. Hair: Well, it's certainly wonderful to have you here. I'm more than glad to participate in this opportunity to do an oral history on the Golden Thirteen for our wonderful Navy.

Starting with my background, I was born in a little place called Blackville, South Carolina, on August 5, 1915, although I didn't know my birth date until just before my retirement. We'll get into that later on. I was born to wonderful parents. My father was a minister and moderator for the Baptist Church in Blackville, and also moderator for the Baptist Church in South Carolina. His name was Reverend Alfred Hair. My mother's maiden name was Rosa Nix. We had 21 brothers and sisters in the family. This came about as the result of two marriages. My father and mother were married previously. And after the deaths of their partners, my mother and father were married. My mother's first husband was named Phoenix.

Going back a little further, my grandparents were in slavery. One of the interesting things about them was that they were sold into slavery after the birth of my father, but the slave master kept my father to raise him. But through some sort of fortune or fate, as it would be, the grandparents were able to be reunited later on in life, and at that time, my father went back to live with them. So that's going back about as far as I know at this time.

Paul Stillwell: When was he born? It must have been before the Civil War.

Mr. Hair: Yes, he was. My father was born in 1851. I took a picture of his tombstone. I don't remember the exact date right now, but he was 72 when he passed away. The reason I remember that is because I am next to the youngest child in the family. I have one brother younger than I am. So many of the children, my sisters and brothers, were grown and married long before I was born. In fact, today I have some nieces and nephews who are older than I am. Of course, I demand that they call me "Uncle Jim" with respect.

Paul Stillwell: How did your father manage to support all those children?

Mr. Hair: In addition to being a minister, my father owned a big farm. There we grew cotton, corn, peas, rice, sugar cane, and other vegetables. The produce from one season usually lasted from one season to another. From this we became very resourceful and learned how to take care of our needs and how to share with others.

Paul Stillwell: You learned how to work at an early age.

Mr. Hair: Yes. Learning responsibility and to share and be resourceful came at an early age. As they used to say in those days, "We need as many hands as we can get," because the fields had to be harvested and the cotton had to be tended. And the children were there to help with the needed jobs which had to be done. I started picking cotton at a very young age with a goal toward being able to pick 100 pounds at an early age. In addition to these jobs in the fields, my parents were both very educationally motivated, which they passed on to the children. In South Carolina, there were several black colleges which my parents often talked about. I believe most of these colleges were started by missionaries, or they were strongly supported by the churches. In Columbia, South Carolina, we had Benedict and Allen colleges. Voorhees and other colleges were nearby. So we came from this mold of being resourceful and at the same time, educationally motivated.

Paul Stillwell: Did you have a very religious upbringing in your family?

Mr. Hair: Oh, yes. My parents were quite religious, which was led by my father, who was the minister of the church. We attended Sunday school, then followed by church services. Between the Sunday school and church services, we had a huge picnic under the beautiful pine trees. This was a big social gathering with a variety of foods which the people often exchanged. This gathering afforded the young single adults the opportunity to do some socializing. This was the only time for socializing due to the work schedule we followed. Other than this, you had to be 21 before you could go out on your own. That's the way it was in those days.

Paul Stillwell: So it sounds as if your parents imparted a strong sense of discipline also.

Mr. Hair: My parents taught that you must do what is right from the beginning. We were taught that there were certain things we had to do each day, and obedience was required at home and in the school. We had to obey our parents, and this same rule applied to our teachers in school. To disobey our teachers was the same as disobeying our parents, and we had to take the consequences—usually a good beating. Hence, they enrolled us in Sunday school, where we learned obedience to God. My parents certainly imparted a strong sense of discipline.

Paul Stillwell: Your parents taught by example, it sounds like.

Mr. Hair: I came up with the belief that example had far more meaning than a lot of preaching. As I said, my father was a minister who was a lecturer and a teacher. He was not the emotional-type preacher. He lectured from the scriptures and according to the scriptures. My mother always supported him in his work and activities. They were not perfect individuals, but the most important thing about them was the example they set for others to follow. I think their example spoke much louder than the preaching.

Paul Stillwell: How much education did he have?

Mr. Hair: I really don't know. But to me he was the most educated man in the world at that time. To me he knew everything. That question came up since I started to do my autobiography, and I am hoping to get some more information to answer that question about my father's education.

Paul Stillwell: He stressed that the children should get an education.

Mr. Hair: Yes, he and my mother. In fact, I don't think my mother could read very well. I know my father could. My mother could read but not fluently. But my mother would always stress to us, "Get those books." My parents were active with the school, Emerson Institute, on all important occasions.

Paul Stillwell: Where was that?

Mr. Hair: Emerson Institute was in Blackville, South Carolina. I don't believe it is there anymore. My parents would never keep you out of school unless you were seriously ill.

Paul Stillwell: They wouldn't let the work in the field get in the way of school?

Mr. Hair: No. No. They would go out and try to do everything, but after school, then you had to go and do your share. You see, you still had your responsibilities. They stressed schooling a lot.

Paul Stillwell: Did you talk with your parents about what sort of career you might go into?

Mr. Hair: No, no, I never got that opportunity to, because . . .

Paul Stillwell: You were pretty young when your father died.

Mr. Hair: Yes, I was still young. I was about eight when my father died. Of course, I was a little older when my mother died. But I never had that opportunity. They would just stress, "Go into education." It wasn't something of telling me what I should do. Of course, reflecting back on it today, had I had the opportunity to have been with my father more, I probably would have ended up being a minister, because he was such an example. But I was only eight when he died, so I didn't have enough of that right at that time. But that was a terrific thing in terms of the background and growing up there in South Carolina.

It was interesting growing up in a secure family there in Blackville. There were two Hair families in this little town—one white and one black. As young children, many of us used to play together when time permitted. With this kind of background, I did not know about racism and discrimination until I was in my teens. There was physical integration in Blackville at that time; black and white homes were next to one another. But the thing that was most meaningful about this was the communication. There was always conversation between the people in the town. When someone got sick, people of all colors came to see the person, bringing food and best wishes. It was a good beginning as a child.

Paul Stillwell: When did you first become aware of the difference between people in terms of black and white?

Mr. Hair: I think I was a teenager when I first became aware of the difference. This was after the death of my father and after we had moved to Florida. We moved to Florida in 1925. After much thought, my mother realized that she could not keep the farm going, because many of the older children had gotten married and moved away. Some relatives had already moved to Florida, and my mother sold the farm and we left Blackville. After being in Florida for a few years, I became aware of the fact that there were no whites living in the neighborhood. Only blacks lived in this area, and there was a demarcation line separating the blacks and whites. This was my awakening to the difference in the races. That's when I really became aware of it, because here we were in a ghetto. All blacks lived in this area, and they had a demarcation line. Maybe it was due to the rural area in South Carolina that had something to do with it, but this was my first awakening to that.

Paul Stillwell: Were there any things in South Carolina that you were prohibited from doing because of your blackness?

Mr. Hair: No, I wasn't aware of it then as a kid. I'm sure there were probably some things, but I didn't know. For example, the man of the white Hair family there was the only undertaker in the town. Of course, he took black and white. So, as I'm saying, I'm sure they had some there, some way or other, but I just was not aware of it as a child at that time. In fact, the white Hairs were relatives of ours. Later on, I know that one of my sisters used to go to visit them, the white Hairs, there in South Carolina. It was that sort of thing. We had quite a friendly relationship.

Paul Stillwell: It must have taken some adjustment, then, when you got to Florida and had to live in this new kind of situation.

Mr. Hair: Well, at that time, you see, I was still a kid, so it didn't bother me that much at that time. But I'm just saying, as I grew up, then I became aware that, "Oh, all of us are living here, and all of them are living over there." The politicians then started drawing up this line of demarcation and emphasizing it in order to be reelected. So you had this sort of thing going on. Plus there were many other things going on there too. But as I say, that was a terrific beginning there in South Carolina. As I said, after my father passed away, then we moved to Fort Pierce, Florida, in 1925.

There again, one of the first things my mother did after getting to Florida was to get us all enrolled in the membership of the church there, Mount Olive Baptist Church. Now, this was a terrific beginning, because we had some outstanding teachers in Florida. One that I always looked up to was our Sunday school superintendent, a guy named Ronald Warrick. He was the shoemaker in the town, but not only was he an outstanding teacher, but the greatest thing about him was his leadership. I guess this sort of goes back to my father. You can preach all you want, but when you can set an example, that's the important thing. And that's the way Ronald Warrick was. He and his wife both were outstanding people. Not only did he teach Sunday school, but his shoe shop was like an open library. He had books there. You could go there, and even though this guy hadn't gone to maybe—I think he said he finished something like seventh or eighth grade, but he could discuss any subject with you. Then it became like an open forum, where we would have discussions about different things.

Paul Stillwell: In the shoe shop?

Mr. Hair: In the shoe shop. Then it was made up of white and black that would come in to these discussions. They were drawn into it, because the discussions were very dynamic and very interesting, and everyone had something to contribute. Aside from this, there were several of us young fellows in this group, but then not only did he let us use his shop there as an open forum for discussions, a lot of times he would lead the discussion. He had on the side of his shoe shop a horseshoe game. When we got tired of the discussion, then we'd say, "Let's go out and play some horseshoe."

Of course, the other thing I liked about him, too, just one of the people that I knew there, and there were several of them, he was a heck of a good fisherman. He would take us out and teach us how to fish. He had one daughter, and she was an invalid, so that took up a lot of his time and his wife's time too. But his wife taught there. When the school was founded, Mrs. Warrick was in the music department, and she wrote the school song. I'm just pointing out a few of these, because these are some of the real people who really were an extension of my parents, in terms of their ideals and their goals and things of that nature. So I could identify with them.

Paul Stillwell: How good an education did you get in those growing-up years, would you say, in retrospect?

Mr. Hair: Oh, it was excellent. It was excellent. Talking about education, I attended Lincoln Park Academy in Fort Pierce, Florida. That's where I completed high school. Lincoln Park Academy, as I recall, was founded in 1925, just the year that we went to

Florida. It was founded as the result of a partial grant—they had some other monies—from the Sears Roebuck Foundation. This is how it got started. There we had some outstanding teachers. They were excellent. One of my favorites was a guy named William Paige. He taught in the science department. His goal was set on teaching, and that's what he did. If you threw a spitball in class or something, if he was demonstrating a science project or teaching anything, that spitball didn't distract Paige. He wasn't going to get caught up in your trouble. And this really took over in that school. This was the emphasis there on education. It was really terrific, but we had a small library. We were limited in that sense. We were limited in certain aspects of the school at this time, but in terms of the basics, we really had a terrific beginning there.

Paul Stillwell: Was there a stress on that as a means of making your way in life, that you had to have that background?

Mr. Hair: Oh, yes. That was a part of it. Education was seen as a means of improving yourself, and through this process you would be able to help others. You gained knowledge so that you would be able to share this knowledge and help others to improve their values in life. Through this education process, we had some outstanding teachers, two of whom I would like to mention, Mr. William Paige and Mrs. Warrick. They were able to establish a consensus between the student and themselves toward an educational goal. There were others who were able to do likewise. I was fortunate to have had so many positive and dynamic teachers. This student-teacher relationship was enhanced due to the ever-present involvement of the parents in the education process.

Paul Stillwell: Did you begin to develop some ideas then of what you might like to do in life?

Mr. Hair: Oh, yes, at that time. I thought about many things. At one time, I thought about becoming a doctor, and I think that was one of my real goals at that time. Just like any high school kid, you get all these ideas, but then when you start getting into college and looking at some of the facts, sometimes you change, and this is what happened to me. But you had high goals. You had high goals of things that you wanted to be.

Paul Stillwell: Well, you had a pretty narrow range of options, though, at that point.

Mr. Hair: Yes. No doubt about it, we did. In line with that, we had a very few schools that we could attend on the collegiate level.

Paul Stillwell: Did you get into athletics and other extracurricular activities in high school?

Mr. Hair: Oh, yes. Oh, yes. I'm glad you mentioned that, because we had a terrific athletic program there. We didn't have football at that time, but basketball was our main thing, and then we got into tennis. In fact, me and two other schoolmates there built the first tennis court on the grounds of Lincoln Park Academy out of concrete. The money was supplied by two black doctors in the town and one black businessman: Dr. Benton, Dr. Rhodes, and Mr. Brown, who was in business. They gave us the money, and we presented the project to them to give us the money, and we went out and did all the work. We had a few other people coming to assist us at times, but we built that first tennis court. Basketball was really outstanding there at Lincoln Park Academy. I still have an old picture here from those days. We had some very competitive teams at that time in high school. One was West Palm Beach, Ocala, and several others were outstanding in basketball. They were really great. West Palm Beach was our greatest rival.

Paul Stillwell: These were all-black schools you played against?

Mr. Hair: These were all-black high schools, because there were no integrated high schools in those days. So one year we would beat West Palm Beach High, and the next year they would beat us. It was that sort of thing. The score was always close, and always a lot of fights in those games.

Mr. James E. Hair, Interview #1 (11/12/86) – Page 10

Paul Stillwell: That's some distance down the coast, so you had some pretty good road trips, I take it.

Mr. Hair: Well, Fort Pierce was only 60 miles north of West Palm Beach. Ocala was a little farther north. We had to play them occasionally.

Paul Stillwell: It's not like playing somebody that's across town, though.

Mr. Hair: No, that's true. And they were enjoyable trips. But we had the all-state tournament there in basketball, which was played up at what we called FAMC—Florida A&M College—at that time.[*] It's a university now, up in Tallahassee. It's a state college.

Paul Stillwell: Jake Gaither.[†]

Mr. Hair: Yes, Gaither. This is where we had our state tournaments every year, and that was a big, exciting thing. Oh, it was great.

Paul Stillwell: How good a player were you?

Mr. Hair: I was on the varsity squad. I was a forward then. I made the varsity team. But in 1936, I guess, my senior year, we went to play in an all-southern tournament, because under the rules, they chose the two best teams from the state. That year Ocala was number one, and we were number two, Lincoln Park Academy. We went to Tuskegee to play in the all-southern tournament, and that was really fabulous.[‡] When we got out there, I think we went up to about the semifinals, and we got eliminated by a team from Bluefield, West Virginia. Oh, they were fantastic. Atlantic Bluefield always came in with some powerhouse teams. But we were giving them quite a battle out there. That

---

[*] A&M – agricultural and mechanical.
[†] Alonzo Smith "Jake" Gaither was head football coach at Florida A&M from 1945 to 1969. In that time his teams compiled a record of 204-36-4 and won six Black College National Championships. He was elected to the College Football Hall of Fame in 1975.
[‡] Tuskegee Institute, Tuskegee, Alabama.

was exciting, and this was my first exposure to a college. That was fantastic. It was almost like going from Hollis to a game down at the Madison Square Garden, to see a big game. That's the way it was in those days at Tuskegee.

Paul Stillwell: It was almost like the Mecca, wasn't it?

Mr. Hair: Oh, yes. It really was in those days. It was really fantastic. Of course, the other thing about that, it was quite a trip. Maybe we'll get into more later on, but with the segregation, the discrimination, and those things, in those days, we had no place to stop off, so we had to drive right on through. Because there was no place you could stop off, no motels or anything in those days, because of the discrimination.

Paul Stillwell: Was that about a day's trip over to there, to Tuskegee?

Mr. Hair: To Tuskegee was more than a day. It was a day and a night almost, especially by car in those days. If you made 45-50 miles an hour, you were doing well, because of the roads. We didn't have good roads. It wasn't that way. Even with all those things, we still made it there, although we had a lot of incidents on the way. But we made it and went on and played in this tournament and had a great time.

But talking about sports and the people there in Florida, Fort Pierce is an outstanding little town. Just like any other town, it's got its good and its bad. But it's an outstanding town. I'll never forget, we had this black doctor that came there, Dr. C. C. Benton. This was during my senior year that he came out and started teaching the fellows how to play football. He just volunteered his time. He was one of these real community-dedicated people. But he didn't take just the kids from high school; he took the fellows off the streets and got them all interested. Everybody was out there, trying to learn this game of football, and they did. From that time on, they developed quite a football team.

With that beginning there, incidentally, sort of carrying this on a little further now and venturing off a little bit, many outstanding athletes have come out of Fort Pierce. Lincoln Park is no longer there now. It was phased out with integration. They have

Westside High. You've got Swoope playing with the Tampa Bay Buccaneers.[*] You got Weathers with the New England Patriots.[†] And you've got Jacqueline Jackson, who is married to Reverend Jesse Jackson.[‡] Her parents were formerly from Fort Pierce during that time, and then she met her husband at North Carolina A&T.

Paul Stillwell: You said you had some incidents during this trip. Had you had enough experience with that in Florida that you knew how to deal with those?

Mr. Hair: Well, I don't know if you ever get to the point to say that you know everything about how to deal with them. There were many, many incidents there on trips. I'll never forget one time. There were towns that no black person was supposed to go into. You don't even know what's happening. For example, one there is Vero Beach, Florida, which was only about 10 miles up from Fort Pierce, but that was a whole town off bounds to blacks. No blacks could stay in Vero Beach. The blacks lived out in a place called Spillway, which was out in back.

One time we were going to Tallahassee, and just as we got there, the car broke down. The school principal and our coach were with us, and I never really had any kind of high regard for our principal as a result of this. In other ways, I guess he was all right. But anyway, as I said, the car broke down, and there was this old huge garage there, like a barracks, one of these big open things where you drive your car into. We managed to get the broken-down car right in front of this garage. So the principal and all of us went in there. It was wintertime. I mention this because we all had on hats and coats. The owner was there having a conversation with another white guy about this car or something, carrying on this conversation, and so this went on and on. Oh, we must have waited a good 45 minutes, just standing there waiting and waiting. He was the boss of this garage, and we had to wait and see him. He was talking about the movie they saw or some social situation, but we had to stand there and wait. Finally he came over, and he said to us, "Look, what are you boys doing in here?"

---

[*] Craig Swoope played professional football for the Tampa Bay Buccaneers from 1986 to 1988.
[†] Robert Weathers played professional football for the New England Patriots from 1982 to 1986.
[‡] Jesse Jackson, a black clergyman and long-time civil rights activist, contended for the Democratic Party's presidential nomination in 1988 before being beaten by Michael Dukakis in a series of primaries.

The principal was an individual who was easily scared, and I guess in a way you could say it was understandable, because in those days some principals felt they had to bow down, or they could have lost their jobs. As long as a white said you were no good, that was it. He insulted you or something. Anyway, he was frightened. This guy came and said, "What are you boys doing here? What are you boys doing here?"

So the principal said, "Sir . . ." And right away the owner recognized this guy was scared. I mean, this is with hindsight that I can look back and say this. But he could see he was frightened, and I knew that he was frightened. He said, "Oh, sir, our car just broke down out here, and we wondered if you would be so kind as to come out and fix this car," really pleading with this guy while shaking. "Oh, if you would just be so kind."

Well, then the guy looked at him and said, "What in the heck you niggers doing in here with your hats on?" Inside this old big, greasy garage. Well, the principal got so frightened that he went around, and before we could take our hats off, which we knew we were going to have to do, he went around and knocked each one of our hats off—bump, bump, bump. Then he looked at him, he was still apologetic. "Oh, gee, I'm very sorry. I'm very sorry, sir, very sorry." He was so frightened.

All of a sudden, this guy looked at the principal and said, "What are you doing with your hat on?" He forgot he had his own hat on. He knocked his own hat off. So I relate this to say that there were many things like this, but it didn't leave a good impression on me about this principal. I said, "Sure, but some time we just have to stand up." I recognized that some time we have to exercise control, but you don't have to be frightened stiff of any kind of situation, especially when you're in a leadership role. Other black leaders would not do that. Where they might have gone along with it and said, "Oh, I see, you want us to take our hats off. All right. Now what's next?" But this guy was really frightened. As I say, outside of that, he was terrific in terms of education and whatnot, but as an example, it just didn't work with me too well.

Paul Stillwell: So this guy would finally fix your car after he had humiliated all of you.

Mr. Hair: Yes, that's right.

Paul Stillwell: Were there any cases where you ever had fear for your personal safety?

Mr. Hair: Oh, yes. Oh, yes. Yes, yes, there were cases on that. Maybe we could go into some of that now. But anyway, it seemed one of the interesting things was there were many times when that would happen—oh, many, many, innumerable times. One of the ones was after the death of my mother, not that that would have stopped it. My mother died in 1933. My sister Margaret was married by then, and I had this wonderful brother-in-law named Estes Wright, who was a most industrious guy. He was a fruit picker by trade, but he was the type of guy that never had to look for a job. He could go out and create a job. I became his shadow. I'd follow him everywhere, because he was really a dynamic individual, very strong. He wasn't afraid of anything or anyone.

One of the greatest things about his wife was her religion. I consider her one of the greatest Christians I've ever met, after I got to know her. Margaret was a very quiet type person, none of this emotional stuff. What aroused my curiosity about her in terms of religion, her beliefs—I used to live with them, and one morning, I had to go to the bathroom. I got up to go to the bathroom, and I heard this noise. It was something like, "Tweet, tweet, tweet." I thought it was a mouse, but I went to investigate. I said, "Gee, this is coming from their room." I tiptoed in to see what it was. This was like 4:00 o'clock in the morning, about 4:00, 4:30, something like that. There she was, up on her knees praying. So after that, I became very curious. And without saying anything to her about it, I observed her. She did this every morning. I don't think her children knew about it. I think I may have mentioned it to them subsequently.

But in terms of your own personal safety, there were many times. Her husband was an outstanding person. He was not in the same vein as she was, in terms of religion, although he was a member of the church, he participated, and that sort of thing. But he was an individual who believed in the dignity and the integrity of the individual, very strongly so. He didn't care what color you were. As I say, I used to shadow him. During that time, the government was giving out surplus foods. It would start like 7:30 in the morning, and they had two lines there.

Mr. James E. Hair, Interview #1 (11/12/86) – Page 15

Paul Stillwell: This was during the Depression.*

Mr. Hair: Yes. They had two lines, one for whites and one for the Negroes. But the Negroes had to wait until all the whites got their share, and then if anything was left, then you would come in and get it. But whenever Estes would go there, he always carried his gun with him, which was a known thing throughout the town. Usually the sheriff was right there. But he would walk in. He carried his burlap bag; he had one and I had one. We'd fill up these bags and put them on our shoulders as soon as the food place opened up, because the stuff was all on the shelves. Then he'd walk by and say, "I got mine," and walk out. The sheriff said nothing. That's the kind of guy Estes was.

Paul Stillwell: He wasn't going to wait in any line.

Mr. Hair: No. I'll never forget another thing. There were so many of these things. For example, there in Fort Pierce—and, by the way, I don't want to sit here and try to castigate Fort Pierce, because these things were happening in many other towns.

Paul Stillwell: Sure.

Mr. Hair: I don't want to say that it was just Fort Pierce, because it was not that way. Fort Pierce had some outstanding people, and I might mention, when I was talking about the athletes, too, another athlete we just had to come out of there was Ed Hearn, who plays for the Mets.† Also, McGriff with the Cincinnati Reds.‡ Although you're a Red Sox fan, I know you've heard of Ed Hearn, who's playing for the Mets.§

---

* Following the crash of the New York Stock Exchange in late October 1929, the United States was plunged into the Great Depression, from which it did not recover until the nation geared up for World War II at the beginning of the 1940s. The Depression was marked by high unemployment and many business failures.
† Edward J. Hearn played major league baseball for the New York Mets in 1986 and the Kansas City Royals in 1987-88
‡ Terry McGriff, who attended Westwood High School in Fort Pierce, later played major league baseball from 1987 to 1994 for the following teams: Reds, Astros, Marlins, and Cardinals.
§ In the 1986 World Series, which was a few weeks before this interview, the interviewer rooted unsuccessfully for the Red Sox against the New York Mets.

But anyway, one of the other things we had there was a law. I don't know whether it was written or not, but it was a law, as far as we were concerned—that no Negro could go down and fish on the bridge at night. We had a bridge that took us right across the Indian River, right to the ocean, a beautiful location. So Estes decided that he was going to do something about it. What he meant by doing something, he was going down to fish at night. I used to trail him everyplace he went. There was the baddest Negro fellow in the town, named Benny Baker. Benny was bad; he was really bad. He was known. He cut up several black guys around there, and he was supposed to be the baddest guy. So Estes went and told him about what he wanted to do: "They don't want us to fish down on the bridge. That's ridiculous. We're paying taxes and everything. That's ridiculous. "I'm going to go down there and fish. What about coming and going with me?"

Benny said, "Let me think about it a little bit."

So Estes said, "Well, look, you don't need too much time to think. But anyway, I'll give you until tomorrow."

He said, "Okay."

So he went back to Benny and found him after going around to several places, and asked Benny. He said, "Benny, what's your decision? You going with us?" When he said, "Us," that included me. I was a kid, and I was going along with this too.

Benny said, "No, man, look, you know, my mother's sick," this and that.

So Estes said, "Oh, forget about it, man. You're chicken. You're chicken. Forget about it." He didn't use "chicken" at that time; he called him something else. I've forgotten now what it was.

But, anyway, the next night, Estes and I went down there fishing. Shortly after we started fishing—we hadn't been there an hour—three white guys came up to us. They looked at Estes. Because I was a kid, see, they all looked at him first. He had a gun, and I had a gun. They said to him, "What in the hell are you niggers doing down here fishing at night?"

Just as soon as he said it, Estes whipped out the .38 and stuck it in his face: "Because we want to." He said, "I'll give you ten seconds to get off this bridge. If I ever see you again, I'll kill you." All three of them took off. Well, we never saw them anymore. They were bullies. We never saw them anymore, but they knew he meant business. That was that. But Estes was a terrific guy. He was the guy that taught me how to handle boats. He taught me all about the water, about the currents, about the wind, the tide, and how you have to use these things.

Paul Stillwell: Where had he picked up all that knowledge?

Mr. Hair: I don't know, but he lived around the water all of his days, so he may have gotten it from his father or something of that nature; I don't know.

Paul Stillwell: It sounds like he was the father that you needed at that point.

Mr. Hair: That's right. He was really something.

Paul Stillwell: He taught you how to be a man.

Mr. Hair: Yes, absolutely. By the way, his mother just died last year; she was 108 years old, there in Winter Park, Florida. But anyway, he was the one that taught me swimming, how to deal with water. There was a group of them, not just me. He had a group of us at that time, taught each of us how to swim in a waterfall. That's when you've really got to be an expert, to know how to swim in a waterfall, because that water keeps pulling you down. But he did all these things.

Paul Stillwell: And you developed into quite a good swimmer, I take it.

Mr. Hair: Oh, yes, a swimmer, and knowing how to handle boats. That's why when I came back—I'm jumping ahead of myself here, but when I came to the Navy, Captain Gill, over here from Third Naval District, asked me about being skipper of a Navy tug.[*] I said, "Sure," because I knew how to handle it already. Estes had taught me, but I guess

---

[*] Captain John M. Gill, USN, was assigned to the staff of Commander Third Naval District in New York City during World War II.

one of the ironies of all of this is the person who taught me all this that I could use in the Navy was lynched in 1935.

Paul Stillwell: Not long after that.

Mr. Hair: That's right.

Paul Stillwell: What was the specific provocation for the lynching?

Mr. Hair: You could have any little thing that might cause it. He was riding downtown. He was going to town, and a friend of his picked him up and said, "Oh, you're walking to town? I'll give you a lift."

"Okay." Just as soon as they got to the beginning of the white section there, here came about six of these white guys, who ran into the car. That was what started it, right there. That was another thing. You used to have it so that if a black man had a new car, I've known them where—I didn't see it, but right up from us, where they locked him with his arms to the steering wheel and set the car on fire. This was the situation of our country in that time.

Paul Stillwell: The fact that Estes wouldn't back down probably made him a high-profile target, and they wanted to go after him.

Mr. Hair: Right. But, anyway, they killed him. Of course, if there is any easy thing about a lynching—the easiest part, if there is anything like that—is the fact that the death comes quickly. Within 15 minutes or so, you're out.

Paul Stillwell: How old a man was he when he was killed?

Mr. Hair: He was a young man. I think he was only in his early 30s. My sister then was expecting her sixth child. But, you see, with lynchings, from my experience of it, the worst part about it is not the lynching itself, the killing, but it's what you have to endure after that, that goes on and on and on, for an indefinite period of time. For example, we couldn't close our door at night, and the police would come into our house at night, night after night.

Paul Stillwell: Why couldn't you close the door?

Mr. Hair: They didn't permit it. See, they were afraid, and they kept us. In hindsight now, they were afraid that we might do something, might escape, maybe get the NAACP to come in on the case.[*] It was out of fear. So you lived through those things, and then you become just completely ostracized from your community. Even all the Negroes around there were afraid. Some of them would come by, and maybe the braver ones would yell across the street, "Hello." They were afraid.

Paul Stillwell: Just because you were related to him.

Mr. Hair: Yes. The whole family.

Paul Stillwell: Did you develop a bitterness over this?

Mr. Hair: Oh, I was most angry about that thing—no doubt about it. No doubt about it. But I'll never forget, though, when this happened, my sister Carrie, who lived just maybe two or three blocks away from where the incident started, came running. I was about seven or eight blocks away, the place where we lived. She came running, and I saw her coming. She started yelling, "James! James! They're killing Estes! They're killing him!" And there she was, yelling to the top of her voice. Well, right away I knew what was happening. By the time you get that kind of message, you know. So I took her on my bicycle, and we rode downtown. At that time, they were taking him to the jailhouse, which was in a long building. Out front were the fire department and a fire truck. In the back was the jail. But when Carrie and I got there, oh, there must have been about 500 or 600 people all gathered around the jail, all white, all white. Not a black person in sight,

---

[*] NAACP – National Association for the Advancement of Colored People.

because it was a frightening thing. But, anyway, we went there, and I parked the bicycle about a block away by a drugstore. My sister and I walked on through the crowd down there, with no one recognizing us, that we were black. I didn't realize that at the time, but now as I look, I'm sure they didn't. Everybody was out just for blood. We walked through this crowd, right on through the fire station to the back, where the jail was. In the jail, they had an old wooden bench, and this is where they had Estes lying, on the bench. All he could do was give these death sounds, the death rattle in his throat—what a hurting sound.

Paul Stillwell: They had cut him down by then.

Mr. Hair: He was gone. But he still had a little breath in him. His heart was still beating. So my sister and I went over to him, and she had a hankie, and we started wiping the blood off his face. His head was soft as cotton, nothing hard about it, like cotton.

Paul Stillwell: So he had been beaten.

Mr. Hair: Oh, yes. At that time, I'm sure none of them ever dreamed that we would come in, and at that time the sheriff, Robert Brown, looked over and he spotted us over there doing something for our brother, and that's what caught his attention. He came over and said, "What in the hell you doing here?"

We said, "We're here to take care of our brother."

He said, "Get the hell out of here right now! Get out!" He was screaming and yelling.

So we started out, and he was following us. As we got out by the fire truck, my sister turned to me and she said, "Look like they would let us do something for him." But he couldn't hear it, so he ran over and he grabbed her by the shoulder and yanked her around.

He said, "What in the hell did you say?"

By that time, I just hauled off and ran right into him with my shoulder—boom!—like a tackle, and knocked him back. There were all these hundreds of people around there. When they saw the sheriff, Robert Brown, knocked back—I didn't knock him all the way down—I had shocked him, and the whole crowd was shocked. He came up and patted me on the head, and he said, "Son, go on about your business." Then my sister and I walked back through that crowd to get our bicycle and go home. That taught me something. It taught me that courage takes over, over any kind of fear you might have. But that was something there, never to be forgotten.

Paul Stillwell: That's obviously stayed with you the rest of your life.

Mr. Hair: I heard someone say that heroism is not just in the battle of the thunder and lightning out on the military fields someplace; it can be anyplace.

Paul Stillwell: That took great courage for the two of you that day.

Mr. Hair: We lived through a lot of that, not just Carrie and I; there were many others. My poor older brother Sam, who was the oldest one in the house at that time, and being the only man in the house, he really had pressure. He was taken out of the house at night, taken away on trips, shifted from one car to another—all that sort of stuff.

Paul Stillwell: Was this just to scare him or what?

Mr. Hair: Yes. Well, not so much to scare him, but to alleviate their fears. It did scare him, no doubt about it, but as I look back on it, they were more afraid than we were, I guess, in those days. But my poor brother Sam, who was an outstanding brother in so many, many ways to all of us, he had so much of that. They'd take him and lock him up in jail, said it was for "safekeeping."

Paul Stillwell: Did you ever have any recriminations after the lynching? Did people bring that up to you, or did they leave you alone?

Mr. Hair: Oh, this went on for months and months after that. It went on for months and months. You were like you were under surveillance all the time, and your friends didn't want to come around, because they were afraid that somebody would talk or some of your friends would try to go get help. This was the thing. Everybody was afraid. A few bad people there took over the whole town. It was that sort of thing, but we had some good people, really good people, on both sides of the fence. But it's what can happen when you get a small number of guys with warped minds in there.

Paul Stillwell: Were you eager to get away from there?

Mr. Hair: No. I never left Fort Pierce because of that. Fort Pierce is a good town, and I could tell you some things about Fort Pierce. It's really outstanding. I still go there almost every year. I have a sister and brother still there. It's a great town. You've got some great people there. People have done a lot to overcome this; they really have. As I say, this could have happened in any town, so I wouldn't want to castigate this town, because it was happening in towns in other states. A lynching could happen in the North, East, South, or West. It takes only a few with warped minds to start a lynch mob. It could happen right here in New York. But good leadership in government and dedicated law officials and good leaders in our institutions serve as a great deterrent to lynch mobs.

Paul Stillwell: But since you personally had been involved, I would think that you would have a reason to want to get away.

Mr. Hair: No. I left Fort Pierce mainly because of the fact of job opportunities. That was my reason, not because of that lynching.

Paul Stillwell: What did you get into after that?

Mr. Hair: Into the field of social work.

Paul Stillwell: What opportunity opened up for you?

Mr. Hair: Well, at that time, you see—if I could, getting a little bit ahead . . .

Paul Stillwell: Well, why don't we just do it chronologically.

Mr. Hair: After that, I remember my brother Sam had a nervous breakdown after being snatched out. All this went on for months. Sam, who was just married, the head of our family, dropped to the floor like a wet dishrag and a body that seemed to have no bone and muscle in it. Somehow he was nursed back, and we sent him to South Carolina to recuperate. When he went down, something inside of me seemed to say, "Now you are the head of the family."

But, anyway, after that, it came time to go to college. I graduated high school, Lincoln Park Academy, in 1936. At that time, my mother was deceased. I enrolled in Bethune-Cookman College at Daytona Beach, Florida, which was a junior college at that time.* This was led by Dr. Mary McLeod Bethune, an outstanding black leader—a terrific person. She was an extension of the type of teaching that my parents had started me out on, like so many other people. So I went there for two years.

Paul Stillwell: How much personal contact did you have with her?

Mr. Hair: I was her office boy, so I saw her a lot.

Paul Stillwell: What do you remember about her personality and her character?

Mr. Hair: Oh, she was a very dynamic person, a very outstanding leader, a person who believed strongly in the dignity and integrity of the individual. She did so much for all of the people of Florida and, later on, the people in the United States, too, because she later became a consultant to three Presidents. She was just an outstanding person. I was glad to have been her office boy.

---

* Mary McLeod Bethune (1875-1955) was a black educator who in 1904 opened at Daytona Beach, Florida, a small school called Daytona Normal and Industrial Institute. It merged in 1923 with Cookman Institute to form Bethune-Cookman College, with Mrs. Bethune as president.

Paul Stillwell: How did that develop? How did you get that position?

Mr. Hair: I was on a scholarship then, so I got there with her.

Paul Stillwell: What sort of course of study did you pursue?

Mr. Hair: Sociology.

Paul Stillwell: You had gotten away from the idea of being a doctor by then?

Mr. Hair: Yes. I was going into sociology, because things were limited then, but I knew I had to get a college degree. That was my aim. But, interestingly enough, before I attended Bethune-Cookman College, I worked. I had earned some money to pay toward my education. I was a soda jerk in a drugstore, plus I did many other things—dig ditches, you name it, anything to make money. So I saved up a few dollars and went to school.

Just before I went to Bethune-Cookman College, I had this job as a chauffeur for a wealthy person there. Next door was this other family, and I got to know the black chauffeur there, a guy named James Stuckey. He was an older fellow, and I got to know him, just as friends, by being chauffeurs; that's all. We'd talk over the fence at times, because these people had quite an estate there, with orange groves in the back and things of that nature. He used to ask me, "What are you going to do with yourself?"

"I'm going to college."

He said, "That's really great. Look, before you go to college, I want you to come by to see me."

So I said, "Okay, Mr. Stuckey, I'll come by." Since he was an older guy then, we always addressed everybody as "Mister" or "Miss."

So I didn't have the slightest—I thought maybe he just wanted to wish me well or something like that. But, anyway, at the termination of my job there, I went over to see him. I said, "Look, I came to say goodbye to you, because I'm going to college now. I've finished my job over here."

He said, "Oh, yeah? Well, come on in with me." This was a very slow, meticulous guy. He must have been in his 60s then or something like that, but he'd been with this family for a number of years. The old man had died, and it was just his wife there—old lady Sidell, we called her. He was still chauffeuring for her. He said, "Come on with me." You can imagine, here I was following James; I didn't know where in the heck he was going. He took me on into the house, led me on into the living room.

I said, "What are you taking me all around here for?"

He went in there, and there was Mrs. Sidell sitting on her sofa. He went over to her, and he said, "Look, I want you to meet James Hair. He is going to college, and I want you to give him some money." Could you imagine? Just right out of the blue! I knew nothing about this. So there I was. I was just about in shock!

So she looked at him, and she said, "James, you know that I don't have any money. Why are you bringing someone here for me to give money to and I don't have any?"

But, anyway, James said, "Yes, you do. I saw the mail today. I saw those checks in the mail today, so I know you have money. Give him some." So they argued there for a while back and forth. He said, "But you do have it. Give it to him."

So she finally consented. She said, "All right." So she turned around, and she got the checkbook, and she wrote me a check for $50.00, which was a heck of a lot of money in those days, in 1936. So she gave me this check. This is something else where I really learned a lesson from James. When she gave me the check, I thanked her for it, and not only did I thank her, but I said to her, "Gee, Mrs. Sidell, as soon as I get out of college and start working, I'm going to pay you this money back."

Well, what did I say that for? Then Stuckey jumped on me. "No! That's a gift! You don't pay somebody back for a gift!" So this went on, and he said, "Don't you pay her a thing. She gave it to you. Didn't you give it to him?"

She said, "Yes."

"Then don't you pay her back. She gave it to you." You learn something every day.

So then I went on to school. I had this $50.00. I said, "Oh, my goodness." I had that in a check, and I said, "I'm going to use this toward my schooling." So I got to

Bethune-Cookman that morning. In those days, we had these great big steamer trunks. Of course, you carried everything in that trunk, heavy as all hell. I got there. I had only about a dollar and a half or $2.00 in my pocket, and I wasn't about ready to try to get a cab or anything like that to take me and my trunks out to school. Now I was wondering how in the heck I was going to get there, because it was something like a mile and a half, a couple of miles to the college. So, anyway, there was this other fellow there. They always had some fellows around there, which I didn't know about. So this fellow came up to me and asked, "Who are you?"

I said, "I'm going to Bethune-Cookman College."

He said, "Good. You are one of our new students."

I said, "Yeah."

He said, "Are you ready to go out to the school?"

I said, "Yeah, but look, I've got my trunk back in there."

He said, "Yeah? All right. Come with me." He took me around in the back there someplace, and they had wheelbarrows in there. I put my trunk in that wheelbarrow, and I rolled it out to the college. So that's how I got it out there. But, anyway, I went on there, and that was one of the greatest times of my life in terms of college experiences. It was a heck of an educational opportunity, and a time where I really got to know a lot. It was an open setting, where you were free to learn, the teachers were really dedicated, really terrific, the librarians and everything else. Many of those same teachers went on. One of my teachers became president of Bronx Community College. He was an outstanding guy.

Paul Stillwell: Why had you decided on sociology?

Mr. Hair: I guess one of the main things was that having seen so many rough things in my life, I guess this sort of shaped my thinking into wanting to do something, if I could, about extending services to people in a way that they could improve themselves. I guess this was true with my father, who was a very helpful person in terms of all the community there in Carolina, when the people got sick or needed this or needed that. So I guess it was a flavoring from this sort of thing, my whole background, and I think this was probably what led me into it. As I said, had I known my father longer, I probably would have become a minister, but I guess that was about what it was.

Paul Stillwell: How did you do in terms of grades?

Mr. Hair: I did all right. I was a good B student, and I was never below a B. My grades were B's and A's. Once or twice I remember getting a C or something like that, but I always stayed up there. But, as I say, that was a two-year college. Then after finishing that, I was hoping to go on to FAMC.[*] But I took a job that summer with a person who had been a teacher there at Bethune-Cookman College, to take care of her home, because she was away that summer. She went away to teach in Alabama and asked me if I'd keep her house for the summer. She had about 400 chickens, 600 pigeons, 20 rabbits, and a couple of dogs.

Paul Stillwell: It was a full-time job.

Mr. Hair: But I took it anyway, and it was one of these things where it was almost self-sufficient. The only thing I had to buy was flour or something like that or meal to make bread. But everything else, I had chickens, I had a vegetable garden there, and all of those things. So she agreed to pay me when she came back, but when she came back, she had other ideas. She said, "Look. What about changing your course and going back to Bethune-Cookman and staying?" Because she wanted me to stay and help, I had done such a good job. She was doing all right with her pigeons, selling squabs, and all that sort of stuff.

But anyway, the gist of it was, I said, "No." Then she got angry with me, and she didn't pay me then. She only gave me enough money for my train fare, and I left there and went to Fort Pierce. So that knocked me out of school for that year. But that didn't stop me. I went up to FAMC anyway. I said, "Let me go up here. Maybe I can convince the president that I'll pay him later or get some kind of scholarship or something." But I went up to FAMC anyway, without having paid any tuition or anything. I must have

---

[*] Florida A&M College in Tallahassee.

stayed there about six weeks, and each day the president would call me in his office, President Lee, and ask me had I gotten the money. He was operating on the basis that my brothers and sisters had a lot, which they didn't have; they didn't have anything. But he was saying that they could afford to pay for my education, and they couldn't. They had their own families. I knew what their situation was, and I wasn't about ready to go out and try to pull from them. But, anyway, after six weeks, I sort of gave up. I said, "Oh, the heck. I'm so far behind in classes now, there's no use staying here." Furthermore, I didn't know if he was ever going to let me in class anyway. So I left and came back to Fort Pierce. One of my friends there helped me bring my trunk down to the station, a very dear friend of mine named Bill Benton. Bill Benton is still there in Fort Pierce today. He became the first black lawyer in Fort Pierce, an outstanding individual. Before that, his father was a doctor there in Fort Pierce.

Paul Stillwell: Is he the one who helped with the tennis courts?

Mr. Hair: Yes, that's right. By the way, these people were very community-minded and had a lot of compassion for people. I don't know if you've heard of Zora Neale Hurston.[*]

Paul Stillwell: No.

Mr. Hair: She was one of the outstanding black women writers, and she was the first black woman to graduate from Barnard College. She and Langston Hughes were contemporaries in that day.[†] But Zora Neale Hurston—and I know I'm probably getting off a little bit now—taught there at Lincoln Park Academy also, but during her last days. Then after that, she became very sick, and she became a pauper. Dr. Benton befriended her, because at this time he had built a lot of small homes out there for people to rent. He let her stay in one of those homes. But I say this: Fort Pierce has a lot of history, a lot of history.

---

[*] Zora Neale Hurston (1891-1960) was a black American writer and folklorist. She was particularly popular during the Harlem Renaissance of the 1920s and 1930s. Her best-known novel was *Their Eyes Were Watching God*, published in 1937.

[†] Langston Hughes (1902-1967) was a black writer in several media: poems, novels, plays, short stories, song lyrics, and newspaper columns. He is best known for his work in the Harlem Renaissance.

Anyway, getting back to my schooling here, I returned home after FAMC. Again, to show you about Fort Pierce, I came back, and I must have walked out two pairs of shoes, just trying to find a job.

Paul Stillwell: The Depression was still on.

Mr. Hair: The Depression was on, and jobs were just hard to come by. So I used to pray a lot, and one day I got this idea. I said, "Heck, I need a job. There must be someone around here who really needs someone to work for them. I've got to continue my education. I'm losing a year already." Time was going by; I still hadn't found a job. Some days I might go out and find a family that I knew needed a ditch dug around the house. I did that. They'd pay you ten cents an hour or something like that. It was the Depression, and things were rough. But, anyway, after praying a lot about this, I got this idea. A lot of wealthy families around there lived on the river. I got this idea to write to one of them, the Peacocks. It was a very candid note. It said, "I am interested in furthering my education. I have completed two years in college, and I need a job to complete my two years. If you have anything available, I'd appreciate hearing."

They didn't write me a letter. They sent one of their servants out to tell me that they had a job and to come on down. Ollie and Mildred Peacock, wonderful people. He has since passed away. She's still hanging on. She's up in age and very feeble now. But, anyway, I went down there and I saw them. They had two servants there, Laura and James. James was the butler and chauffeur and everything else, and Laura was mainly the cook. They told Laura and James about it and asked, "What about it?"

James said, "Oh, yes, I'd be glad to. I can just take care of the yard then, and let him be the butler and chauffeur." Something like that.

I went down, and I became the chauffeur and the butler. Anyway, I had a job, so I worked there for about a year, and I saved up my money. In the meantime, I was trying to get into school. I had written to several schools, but then after finishing up my job with them, it was still the summer before I went to school, so I went to Atlantic City. After walking out a lot of shoes there, I finally got a job as a short-order cook. I didn't know anything about cooking, but I learned right quick. Anyway, the reason I mention that, going back to Florida that year, this same fellow that I knew before, James Stuckey—I was telling you about the chauffeur—his family was from Atlantic City. So until we could get work, there was a group of us, we could go by there, and they'd give us food.

Paul Stillwell: At the Sidells' place.

Mr. Hair: Yes, that's right. Through James and the cook there. Old Lady Sidell knew this. She didn't mind. But, anyway, James had a car of his own, and he asked me if I'd drive it down to Florida. I said, "Yes." I took about four or five guys with me, and we went on down. When we got there in Georgia someplace, I had a flat tire, no spare. So I said, "Oh, what am I going to do?" I got out and started to try to hitch a ride to town to get this spare fixed. Along came this fellow in this big, brand-new Buick, one of those big cars, and he had a young fellow in there with him, must have been a fellow about 18, and this was an older fellow. So they stopped and asked me where was I going. I told them I had a flat tire, and I wanted to go down to the next town here to get it fixed and wondered if they'd give me a lift.

They said, "Yeah, sure. Jump in the back."

Great big car, so I got in the back. He asked me about all what I was doing. I told him, "I'm going back to college."

"Which college?"

"I don't know yet. I applied to several of them. I'm waiting. I'm going to one of them anyway. I'm that kind of a determined guy."

So anyway, so we got there, and we got out, and he said, "Look. Okay, get your tire fixed, and we'll take you back out there."

It wasn't far, about a mile or so out of town. So I said, "Great." And I looked up, and he was wearing this white collar, and then I realized, maybe this was a Catholic priest, because I knew nothing about Catholicism at that time. It turned out, he was. I told him I was going to any one I could think of.

So he said, "What about trying Xavier University in New Orleans?"

I said, "I'll try any of them." So I sent an application in, and apparently he wrote a letter or something for me. Anyway, I was accepted out there.

Paul Stillwell: A little thing like that.

Mr. Hair: That's right. One unusual thing about Xavier, then they wrote and asked me for pictures and all that sort of stuff, which I gladly sent, because I was anxious to get an education.

I went out there. Of course, this opened up a new world of learning to me, because I'd never witnessed anything like this before. I'd been in an open setting, where you were free to learn, free to challenge anything in an educational sense. Out there it was completely different. It was run by some nuns, whom I had never been around before in my life, and they controlled everything. One day, I went to the library to get some books. Some new books had just come in, and I wanted one of those books, but they said, "No, we have to wait until the good sisters read it." Then they would decide whether we could read it.

Paul Stillwell: Censorship.

Mr. Hair: So they could be sure there wasn't anything there that endangered your mind. Now, this was a shock, because with Mrs. Bethune, when I walked in the library there, or any student, they said, "What subject do you want?" You were free to learn. Out there it wasn't that kind of open education. That just shocked me. I said, "Oh, my God! What have I gotten into?" But at the same time, I said, "I've got to keep my mind on my goal." I didn't have many opportunities as it was, and I was on a scholarship there, too, working my butt off.

Paul Stillwell: Doing what?

Mr. Hair: I was in the recording office, where you worked every afternoon after school—worked from 4:00 to 6:00 or 7:00, something like that, and then you worked on Saturday.

Paul Stillwell: Was this for the registrar?

Mr. Hair: Yes. Plus then I had a job down at the Jung Hotel at night, like 7:00 to something, working in the cocktail lounge. I was a porter in the cocktail lounge, which meant I wouldn't get home until about 3:00 o'clock in the morning.

Paul Stillwell: Tough to study then too.

Mr. Hair: Oh, yes, it was. Yes. But now this was my scholarship. I was working my butt off. I didn't have much time for socializing. But the other learning thing for me, too, was there was this girl in class, and I remember her. Oh, I liked her. She was a beautiful doll; she was really beautiful. One of those Cajun gals, really beautiful. So I was trying to get to know her. We sat opposite one another, and occasionally I would talk to her. "What's your name?" and things of that nature. Then later on, I started, "I'd like to come and see you sometime. Would that be all right with your parents?" In those days, you had to get permission from the parents to go around socializing with any gal. She kept putting me off, putting me off for some reason, and here I was. I was completely naive to these sorts of things. So this went on and on.

One day she came into class and said, "Hello." She was very friendly this day.

We started talking, and I thought, "Oh, boy, this gal is really getting to like me, man. I'm something." So what topped off, then she asked me if she could have one of my pictures. I said, "Oh, yeah, sure." I didn't have any pictures then, but I finally got myself ten cents and ran out and had some pictures made. I went back in, my chest all stuck out, and gave it to her, not realizing that the reason she wanted it was to take it to her parents to see if I was fair enough to pass, because they had that terrific class system. It was really something. I noticed some other schools had this, too, but New Orleans was really something else. This was a terrific learning thing, plus many other things.

But, anyway, I made it through there. I'll never forget, though, before I left, I had become the secretary to the dean of religious studies, meaning that in addition to all these other jobs I would do, I would keep the class attendance. This person was a most influential person. He had written books.

Paul Stillwell: What was his name?

Mr. Hair: An outstanding speaker. When he'd come to New York, Ed Sullivan would take him on the show like that.* His name was Father Murphy. I kept this class roll. He was from Boston or someplace. But like this black principal I told you about that we had in Fort Pierce, Father Murphy also didn't leave me with a good impression. There were a couple of things that happened, and one was that since I was in the recording office, I was writing for the dean and everybody. I was in with the group. They had a lot of trust and a lot of confidence in me, because two of us there were taking care of the grades of all the students, transferring from the teachers' rolls to the cards. But one day, the school choir, which was an outstanding choir, was going down to Roosevelt Hotel, which was the leading hotel there in New Orleans. The war was just started, and Douglas Fairbanks Sr. was on this program.†

Paul Stillwell: In person?

Mr. Hair: Yes, in person. Plus they had some other movie stars there, but Douglas Fairbanks was the leading figure. Then they were bringing in the Xavier choir. Oh, my God, a time to see a real good show. So I got talking it up around there in the recording office to the dean and everybody. Finally, I said, "Gee, I'd love to go to that."

They said, "You would?"

I said, "Yeah."

"Look, you can get in with the choir."

---

* Ed Sullivan was a popular New York newspaper columnist. He was later host of "The Ed Sullivan Show," which was the longest running variety series in television history, 1948-71.
† Douglas Fairbanks Sr. (1893-1939) was an American movie actor, director, and producer. He is best known as a swashbuckling character in the silent-film era.

"But I can't sing."

"Well, just fake it." Because I could never make a joyful noise. But, anyway, I got in with this choir, and Father Murphy was taking the group. He was our chaperone. We all got in this bus, the choir, me, everybody. There must have been about 50 of us and Father Murphy. We drove down and stopped right in from of the Roosevelt Hotel. Father Murphy had the driver to stop, and then he got up and said, "All right, now. We're here now, but I want you to stay right here in the bus. I'm going to go on in, but the driver will take you around to your entrance." Sure enough, he did. He took us around to the freight elevator in back of the hotel.

I said, "Oh, my God." So, like I say, neither one of these two left me with a good impression. I realized what the situation was in those times, but do you really have to do this? We didn't have to go. Had I known this, I wouldn't have gone.

The other thing there that really got me, I was quite a student. I used to be one of these eager beavers when it came to studying. In fact, when I was in high school, they promoted me twice in mid-term. Not because I was a genius or anything like that, but I loved studying, and I would stay ahead. So when the teacher got ready to make an assignment for a week in advance, she would sometimes ask, "Who knows something about this particular subject?" or "Who knows what this is about?" I'd give them the answer, so they thought, "This guy's a genius." And they would promote me, but that was no good, because it put me completely out of my age group. Then I started playing hooky so I could get back with my group.

But, anyway, before I graduated from Xavier, I had more than the required 132 credits, or something like that. I had far more than that, because I had an excess when I went there from Bethune-Cookman College, because I loved to study. Instead of 132, I must have had at least 145 credits. But while I was there, I had taken some advanced courses in sociology. This was over and above the college level, which was a special program that they offered there at the school. Therefore, Father Murphy knew all about this, not that he was monitoring our class or anything like that. But anyway, just before my graduation, he came to me and asked me what was I planning to do. I said, "As you know, I've been taking these advanced courses in social work. I hope to go into the field of social work when the opportunity arises. That is, if I have any more time before going into the service." Because, you see, I was in the first draft, 1941.

Paul Stillwell: Was that the year that you got your degree?

Mr. Hair: I got my degree in 1942. I was drafted in 1941, but I got an educational deferment for one year.

As I said, he asked me about what was I planning to do, and so I told him at that time I certainly wanted to go in the field of social work. I said, "That's the profession I want to follow."

He said, "Oh, good, because I know the commissioner here in the Department of Welfare. Maybe I can get you in there," which I'm sure he could. He was a most influential person. He had written books. Ingrid Bergman was said to play the leading role in a movie that was to be made from his book *The Scarlet Lily*. But that didn't come off, because at that time she got a divorce, and you know how that was in those days.[*]

Paul Stillwell: Right.

Mr. Hair: Anyway, so he said he knew the commissioner, which I knew he did, a most influential person. He had a golden tongue and could speak eloquently. He said, "Well, I'll look into it."

I said, "Oh, great. Thanks a lot, father. I really appreciate that. That's just the field that I want."

He came back about two or three days later, and he said, "Look, I talked with the commissioner, and you got the job."

I said, "Oh, great! That's wonderful, father! Gee, how can I thank you?"

He said, "Well, now, I'll tell you. It's like this. You see, you can get the job, but what he wants you to do first is come to his home and work, taking care of his yard. Then if he likes you, then you can have the job."

---

[*] In 1950 Swedish-born film star Ingrid Bergman divorced her first husband in order to marry director Roberto Rosellini.

Paul Stillwell: That's a strange setup.

Mr. Hair: I said to myself, "Oh, my God. You're going into the category of this frightened principal I had." So the gist of it was, I told him, "No, thank you, father. I'll think of something else."

So I think this sort of reflects on what our country was like in those days, irrespective of any town. This happened in so many places.

Paul Stillwell: So he had told the guy you were black, then, obviously.

Mr. Hair: Oh, yes. Oh, yes. He knew that. I'm sure the commissioner knew many people, but I'm sure he told him that I was black. He wouldn't have pulled anything like that on the commissioner, I'm sure of that.

Paul Stillwell: But he wanted to see if you were a "good black" before you got the job.

Mr. Hair: That's right. Absolutely. Absolutely. So anyway, with that, I was graduating around June the first of 1942.

Paul Stillwell: The war had started by then.[*]

Mr. Hair: As I said, I was in the first draft after Roosevelt started pulling those names out of the barrel.[†] I got my notice. But fortunately, I got an educational deferment.

So just before I graduated, about a couple of weeks before then, I got my letter to report on July the first, 1942. I said, "Oh, yes." But I never wanted to go in the Army. Of course, there were many reasons for this, basically because Estes had taught me so much about the water, and I loved the water, and I knew a lot about the water. Furthermore, I didn't like the color of the Army's uniforms. As we used to say in those

---

[*] The United States was pulled into World War II when Japanese naval forces attacked the U.S. Navy base at Pearl Harbor, Hawaii, with carrier planes.
[†] Franklin D. Roosevelt was President of the United States from 1933 to 1945.

days, it reminded me of shit. But anyway, I was gung ho for going in the Navy. No doubt. I had made up my mind.

Paul Stillwell: The Navy did not have a good reputation among blacks at that time.

Mr. Hair: No, not at all. Not at all.

Paul Stillwell: You were going in anyway.

Mr. Hair: But I was aware of what many of the black churches, Mrs. Bethune, and the NAACP, were doing to try to get the Navy to change their policies. I knew, because I had had personal contact with Mrs. Bethune, and I knew through that what she was doing with the Roosevelts, as one of his aides.* I had to go in, although they hadn't been good toward Negroes at that time in either branch of the service. I knew I had to go in for the good of my country, so I was going to go in. But I wanted the Navy. I wanted the best that I could get in the Navy, so I decided then, "Well, I've got a few more days in New Orleans before I go in." This was maybe a week or two before time to go in, something like that. So I decided I'd explore around and see what the possibilities were. I went down to the Navy recruiting office there in New Orleans. I walked in. They had all these pamphlets out, and I was looking all around. At that time, there was a lot of competition going on between the Army and the Navy to get guys into the service. There was a rivalry going on between them. There was a white recruiting officer there, and I'm sure he knew that I was black.

Paul Stillwell: Were you ever mistaken for white?

Mr. Hair: Oh, that has happened to me. That has happened. As I told you about the lynching thing, I'm sure they didn't recognize me, because at that time it was a different

---

* President Roosevelt's wife Eleanor knew Mrs. Bethune and was an active proponent of expanded opportunities for black citizens.

sort of thing altogether. Nobody would ever suspect that any black would come around there at that time.

But, anyway, so this recruiting officer came over to me. He said, "Gee, I'm glad to see you. Thinking about the Navy?"

I said, "I sure am."

He said, "Oh, well, look, come on right over here." He started patting me on the back and said, "My little French boy, come on in and sign up."

Paul Stillwell: He thought you were a Cajun.

Mr. Hair: No! I think he knew what I was.

Paul Stillwell: I see.

Mr. Hair: But he, I guess, in his way was being sympathetic towards me, because he realized what the situation was toward Negroes. So your best chance was to get in as something else, and then you would go in under general enlistment.

Paul Stillwell: So the general service had not opened up for Negroes then.*

Mr. Hair: No. Not then. Not then, see, but they were still working on it. Because what they had then, you see, all Negroes just went into the mess branch, and I think some of them, there might have been a few in the machinists, maybe just a handful or something like that. But basically it was not open up to us at that time.

Paul Stillwell: Right.

Mr. Hair: But, anyway, I said to him, "This really sounds great, but I need a few days. I've got to go back and get some of my things straightened out and think about it, but I'll

---

* The change that permitted entry by black enlisted men into the Navy's general service ratings became effective in June 1942.

be back down here, don't worry. I'll be back." Placating this guy along. So, heck, I left then. Then I went back and got my trunk and everything ready. I left there, and I went to Florida. Then I heard about this new program that the Navy had just started, whereby they had taken blacks, generally from the field of education, and made them recruiters. They'd take them from schools and colleges. I heard about this, so I went. They had one that was recruiting out of Jacksonville, Florida, and I went there to see this person. There was a fellow by the name of Alexander. I've forgotten his first name. That's where I met this Mr. Alexander.

Paul Stillwell: So I guess he was in the same category that Dennis Nelson was.*

Mr. Hair: Yes. He was a recruiter. Then he told me about this open enlistment program, whereby I could go in as what they called then an able-bodied seaman, into the general enlistment program. Very intelligent man, and I was most impressed with him. I could see that he wasn't giving me anything but the truth. He was very honest and open, very candid. So I told myself, "I like this." They could swear you in

Paul Stillwell: When did you enlist?

Mr. Hair: July 1, 1942. So he sent us on to Great Lakes, to Camp Robert Smalls, for boot training.†

Paul Stillwell: What do you remember about that period? A lot of marching, undoubtedly.

Mr. Hair: Oh, yes, no doubt about it.

---

* Dennis Denmark Nelson II later became a member of the Golden Thirteen.
† Recruit training, known more commonly as boot camp, was conducted at the Naval Training Station, Great Lakes, Illinois, about 30 miles north of downtown Chicago on the shore of Lake Michigan. Within the Great Lakes Naval Training Station, Camp Robert Smalls was the site of training for black recruits. It was named for an escaped slave who captured the Confederate steamer *Planter* during the Civil War and turned her over to the U.S. Navy.

Paul Stillwell: What sort of curriculum and training did you have there?

Mr. Hair: That was really quite some training up there. Terrific boot camp training. It was rather easy for me because of my athletic background. I mean, the physical aspect of it, going through all the obstacle courses and all those different courses that we had to go through. That was easy, mucking across all this water. That was all easy, because physically I was in great shape.

Paul Stillwell: I'm sure the classroom work was easy, too, because it was not geared for college graduates.

Mr. Hair: No, no. It wasn't bad. You see, after boot came your classroom. Because then I went into quartermaster school after the boot camp training.[*]

Paul Stillwell: Why did you want to be a quartermaster?

Mr. Hair: That's a good question. They had several things there that you could do, and I wasn't inclined in a mechanical way. I guess the main thing was that I liked being on top of a ship anyway, up above, as opposed to down below. I knew this was an area where I could be. So I just chose to go into quartermaster school.

Paul Stillwell: Was it a tie-in at all with the boat handling and the navigation?

Mr. Hair: I imagine it was. I imagine it was tied into that. I haven't thought about it in that sense, but I'm pretty sure it was.

Paul Stillwell: Did you say that Charles Lear was there at the same time you were at boot camp?[†]

---

[*] The Navy's enlisted rating of quartermaster is one that specializes in navigation.
[†] Charles Lear was an enlisted man who later became a member of the Golden Thirteen.

Mr. Hair: I think he was, but I didn't know him personally then. As I recall, I saw him on a few occasions, but that was about it.

Paul Stillwell: How sympathetic or cooperative would you call the people who were running the boot camp, your chief petty officer in your company, and so forth?

Mr. Hair: It varied. Some of them were very good. They were outstanding leaders in the camp. Most of them were white men. I can remember one I had that was really a quite outstanding fellow, and he was a good leader, all military, and stuck right to it. That was it. But there were some others who were not good. I remember one guy who was in another company, and he'd been there for quite a while. Everybody talked about Wallace. I think that was his name. I remember the time when he had many companies in training. Finally, one day Wallace got his orders to go out with one of the companies.* Nobody liked Wallace. Wallace was cruel. He was still very much a racist. But Wallace got his orders to go out with this company. They used to have these little graduation ceremonies for the barracks. Usually, your company commander would get up and say good things about you: "Go get 'em, fellows," and blah, blah, blah—gung ho this sort of stuff. So Wallace got up that night. He knew he had to go out with his company, and the guys were around there saying, "Oh, we're going to kill this guy. All we've got to do is get him out to Eniwetok."† He was going out with one of these supply companies. There was all kind of talk. They hated Wallace for all the things he had done to them.

Well, Commander Armstrong was sitting up there with all these officers.‡ Wallace got up there and he said something to the effect that, "Look, fellows, we've done a good job here in boot training, and so we're going out. But before we go, I want all you niggers to know I don't want no shit out of you." Well, the guys flew into a rage. I'll tell you, it was a scramble out there with Wallace. Wallace got his orders; he was gone after that. I never saw Wallace anymore after that. But you ran into some things like that.

---

* "Going out" in this sense means leaving the training environment and going to a substantive duty assignment, perhaps at an advanced base. Wallace was clearly reluctant to continue to serve with black sailors.

† Eniwetok is an atoll in the Marshall Islands. U.S. forces captured it in early 1944.

‡ Commander Daniel W. Armstrong, USNR, was officer in charge of Camp Robert Smalls. He was a 1915 Naval Academy graduate who resigned his regular commission after World War I and was recalled to active duty for World War II.

Mr. James E. Hair, Interview #1 (11/12/86) – Page 42

Paul Stillwell: Did you think Armstrong was a good man?

Mr. Hair: I didn't really know Armstrong. It's an interesting thing that happened, because I just knew of him, and I guess I knew more about him through Goodwin.

Paul Stillwell: Goodwin was really the link.*

Mr. Hair: Oh, yes. You hate to judge a person, I would say, on just what you hear and that sort of thing. Goodwin was that link.

Paul Stillwell: He's not around anymore, so maybe you can tell me some of the things that he passed on. Did Goodwin feel comfortable about him?

Mr. Hair: Yes, I think so. You see, the reason why I mention Goodwin was that he did a terrific service during that time, because you have to picture how the country was in those days, in terms of races. During those days, Commander Armstrong and the white officers there needed this link, and Goodwin supplied this link.† Therefore, it was more or less what Commander Armstrong wanted, this sort of thing—good military discipline. But to know him personally, I never really got to know Armstrong that way. You know what I mean?

Paul Stillwell: Yes.

Mr. Hair: But Goodwin was this link, and because he served in that role, I'm sure there were a lot of people that didn't think too highly of Goodwin being in that role.

Paul Stillwell: Do you mean people in the Golden Thirteen or elsewhere?

---

* Reginald Ernest Goodwin was an enlisted man who later became a member of the Golden Thirteen. He served in Armstrong's office before being selected for officer training.
† Goodwin served as a liaison person and communication link between the white officers and black sailors.

Mr. Hair: I mean people around the camp. And yet there were some who [unclear] him. I just didn't know him, but I knew Goodwin was in that role. One of the sad parts about it was that Goodwin felt so close to Armstrong. This really came through to me very clear. In fact, he used to talk about it, that he wasn't going to have to go out to the Pacific, because Commander Armstrong couldn't do without him. He was his aide. This was the impression Goodwin gave. These were the things he talked about.

Paul Stillwell: Sort of a teacher's pet type.

Mr. Hair: Yes, that's right. So Goodwin, as I said, had this relationship. I knew him in our class, which was all study, study, study, study.* Of course, he would correct us when we got out of line any time. For example, I remember one time, I said in everything there's got to be some kind of tranquility, or you've got to have some kind of [unclear] or something.

Paul Stillwell: Got to have some relief from the pressure.

Mr. Hair: That's right. So I'm pretty sure it was me, but one day I suggested to the group—one night—we were spending every day and every night, when we were not in class, we studied. We were up late at night in the head there, something up to the window with the light on, which we weren't supposed to do. We would grill one another on different subjects. So anyway, I suggested a little break. I said, "Hey, let's shoot some dice." Well, somebody there had a pair of dice; I don't remember who it was. So we got down for pennies, just to break the monotony, ease the pressure. We got down and started shooting dice for pennies. "Come on, come on." Goodwin was in the head when we got this game together. All of a sudden, Goodwin came out of that head, and he saw us down there on our knees, shooting dice. "Fellows! Fellows! What's going on here? Look here. You are officers! Down there on your knees, shooting dice! I cannot take this. Stop it, or I will report you."

---

* This refers to the officer training class in early 1944 that comprised 16 officer candidates, including Hair and Goodwin.

We said, "Yes, sir. Yes, sir, Mr. Goodwin. Yes, sir." We knew he wasn't kidding. And we placated Goodwin. "Oh, gee, sorry. We weren't gambling; we were just playing for fun," and all that sort of stuff. But no more dice. Not any. We knew. We knew. We had to walk the line.

Paul Stillwell: You couldn't afford to take chances.

Mr. Hair: Not at all.

Paul Stillwell: That's really jumping ahead. Maybe we ought to cover your enlisted service before we get you into the officer period.

Mr. Hair: Okay. By the way, just a little side thing regarding my boot camp, I had my Lincoln Park Academy, my LPA high school ring, and during all the calisthenics we had to take, you'd have to take them off, because they'd cut your hand. So there was this very good friend of mine I met in camp, a guy named Smith. I've forgotten his first name; I think it was H. Smith. So I asked him to hold my high school ring until I finished, because he had completed the course. He said, "Okay. I'm going on back to the barracks."

I said, "Well, I'll get it later."

"Okay." So he held my ring. I went through these calisthenics courses. Anyway, when I got back there, I didn't see him that night. The next day, I was looking around for Smith. I couldn't find him anyplace. Come to find out, Smith decided he would sneak out and see some girls that night with a group of fellows, like some of the guys would do. He got caught, and they shipped him out. I never saw Smith or my ring since. But anyway, that's just a little aside.

Paul Stillwell: The fortunes of war.

Mr. Hair: Yes. But I really missed that ring, though. Anyway, so I finished boot camp, and after that I went into quartermaster school there. That was an interesting school.

They taught you a little bit of everything in there, not only just navigation, everything, signaling, plus plane spotting, a lot of different kinds of things. But one of the things was, in the gunnery class, in the gunnery part of it, I'll never forget, because at that time, we didn't have any guns. They wouldn't let us walk guard but with an empty gun. You couldn't carry a gun, a loaded gun, or anything like that.

Paul Stillwell: Just blacks couldn't, or all the boots?

Mr. Hair: No, no. I don't know whether it was all or not, but I'm pretty sure. It was that way with us. That was a problem, because for a long time, even in the Army, before they decided to give blacks guns. I think the same thing was probably true there at Great Lakes. But anyway, that school was very, very interesting and very good.

Paul Stillwell: Was that segregated?

Mr. Hair: Oh, yes. Everything was at Robert Smalls, which was a segregated camp altogether. But I completed that course, and after finishing boot camp, I came out of there as quartermaster third class. Then I was sent to Third Naval District here in New York. Then I went onto this tugboat, the USS *Penobscot*.*

Paul Stillwell: When did that happen? How long had your period at Great Lakes been?

Mr. Hair: What was that school? I have trouble remembering the exact amount of time, but I think boot camp was what, six weeks or something like that?

Paul Stillwell: Probably.

---

* USS *Penobscot* (YT-42) was a 122-foot, 415-ton harbor tug that the Navy had acquired in 1917. For many years she served in New York Harbor. She was scheduled to be retired in 1939 but remained on active service because of worsening world conditions. In May 1944 she was redesignated YTB-42 and continued duty until 29 October 1945, when she was placed out of service.

Mr. Hair: And the school was maybe ten weeks, 12 weeks, something like that, and then it was early '43 when I went aboard that ship.

Paul Stillwell: Was she operating in the port of New York?

Mr. Hair: Yes, port of New York. We served New York then. At that time, we were putting up nets along with the engineers and whatnot, steel nets adjacent to Ambrose Channel, which comes into New York.

Paul Stillwell: For protection against submarines?

Mr. Hair: Yes, protection against submarines. We had those nets on both sides of Ambrose Channel. That was a very difficult job. I did most of the steering of the boat at that time.

Paul Stillwell: Did it have an all-black crew?

Mr. Hair: No, these were all integrated. In fact, all the ships I've been on were integrated, come to think of it. All of them integrated. Although the *Mason*, we'll get into that.

Paul Stillwell: Just barely.

Mr. Hair: It started out to be all black, but it never really got that way.

But the interesting thing about the *Penobscot* was that the nets were right here that we had to work on, and about 200 feet behind, you had all these mines that were laid, that were TNT. So you had to really be careful in maneuvering in there, although we had the boats depermed, with the hope of not being magnetic.*

---

* Deperming is a process by which a ship's permanent magnetism is reduced by energizing coils placed temporarily around her. The purpose is to make her less susceptible to magnetic mines and torpedoes.

Mr. James E. Hair, Interview #1 (11/12/86) – Page 47

Paul Stillwell: So they were magnetic mines?

Mr. Hair: Yes. Right. But that, we had to really be careful. So we worked on that, plus we did a lot of towing, we did a lot of docking, assisting ships in docking.

Paul Stillwell: Do you remember any highlights, any specific incidents from your time in the *Penobscot*?

Mr. Hair: Like what were you thinking of?

Paul Stillwell: Say, a damaged ship that you brought in, or something really interesting in net laying.

Mr. Hair: That we would assist on. We had many of them. Like I remember the USS *South Dakota*.

Paul Stillwell: She had been badly damaged in the South Pacific.*

Mr. Hair: So we had many ships, some ships that had been wrecked. Once we had a destroyer that just blew right up, right out here in Ambrose Harbor. It was anchored out there. Something went wrong, and a fire started down in the ammunition room, and the whole mast and everything—that ship sank right out there. We worked with the old *Kearsarge*, which was the biggest ship with a crane on it.†

Paul Stillwell: Was she over at the Brooklyn Navy Yard?

Mr. Hair: Yes, she was.

---

* The battleship *South Dakota* (BB-57) was damaged by Japanese gunfire in the Naval Battle of Guadalcanal, 14-15 November 1942. On 18 December 1942 she arrived at the New York Navy Yard in Brooklyn for repairs and overhaul. The repairs were completed, and she was back at sea 25 February 1943.
† USS *Kearsarge* (BB-5) was commissioned as a battleship on 20 February 1900. She was decommissioned 10 May 1920 for conversion to a crane ship. She was designated *Kearsarge* (AB-1) on 5 August 1920. On 6 November 1941 she lost her name for use in a new aircraft carrier and became known simply as *Craneship Number 1*. She was eventually sold for scrap in 1955.

Paul Stillwell: That's where the *South Dakota* went in also.

Mr. Hair: Yes. But out there, we were trying to salvage this ship that had sunk. We were trying to do something with it. Then we worked down around Earle, New Jersey, where they had an ammunition dump.

Paul Stillwell: So it was potentially hazardous work.

Mr. Hair: No doubt about it. You could get blown up. But it was a great thing, though, to be able to get out there and maneuver out there with all those ships. It really requires a lot of skill to be able to do that.

Paul Stillwell: How were you treated by the other members of the tug's crew?

Mr. Hair: Oh, great, great. That was one of the interesting things about it. I guess it was like a phenomenon, I guess, in terms of integration in the services. The most amazing thing, I guess it's the idea of patriotism. Not that everybody was this way. I mean, you ran into your radicals and whatnot, but, by and large, I was very fortunate. When I later went to China, I had a lot of trouble then. But by and large, here it was really great. One of the interesting things was—I know I'm jumping around a little bit—here I was just an enlisted man, you know, still just a sailor, an enlisted man.

But one of the interesting things, along the same line, when I became an officer and went aboard the ship, I had an integrated crew, and they were just great. But to me, one of the things that seemed to influence them so greatly was your skills in handling that boat. Because here you were working in dangerous areas. They knew those mines were right there. If you foul up, not only you go under, you're going to get somebody else killed, too, you know, so you've had it. Plus, we had a fire down there around [unclear] one night and tried to put that out. Things of that nature. A tanker or something caught on fire. What a blaze—that thing was billowing like mad. We went in there to try to put it out, assist in it because this other ship was trying to do the same thing. But after you go through these things with your crew, they really develop a lot of respect for you.

Paul Stillwell: It builds a bond.

Mr. Hair: Yes.

Paul Stillwell: Because you depend on each other.

Mr. Hair: That's right.

Paul Stillwell: What rank was your skipper?

Mr. Hair: The first skipper I had on the *Penobscot* was a chief warrant officer, and then after that, a lieutenant (j.g.).[*] That was the highest.

Paul Stillwell: Were they supportive of your efforts? Any prejudice on their part?

Mr. Hair: Oh, no. No, they were very supportive. I didn't run into any prejudices with them. You know, a very interesting thing happened with me; this was after I became an officer. No, while I was still enlisted. We used to get officers to come over occasionally, an ensign, a lieutenant (j.g.), or sometimes a lieutenant, and I never will forget, once we had this lieutenant to come by, and they would come by for training. They would sit there and watch us, what we were doing, how we'd handle the ship, and so forth. Then the next thing I knew—one of these officers used to get assignments like taking ships to other places, and this was like a plum job. They used to love that. Well, this one, Lieutenant Jensen, got an assignment that was to take this torpedo tender to Gulfport, Mississippi, but the first thing he did was to go and ask for James Hair to be his quartermaster. Now here we go. That was the only ship I was on where I was the only black person on the ship. So we took this ship down to Gulfport, Mississippi.

Paul Stillwell: Do you remember the name of it?

---

[*] J.G. – lieutenant (junior grade).

Mr. Hair: It was the *LCS-71* or something like that.* But we took that. That was really a terrific, terrific trip that we had down there. Most of it was through inland waterways, which was terrific. I'm sure that's why he took me along, because I knew how to navigate the waterways. So that was about the extent of my enlistment as a quartermaster assigned to those ships.

Paul Stillwell: Where did you live when that ship was in port?

Mr. Hair: We stayed right aboard the ship. We stayed right aboard it the whole time.

Paul Stillwell: How big was the crew?

Mr. Hair: We had about 25 or 30 people aboard those tugs. That's about what they carried. We all lived right aboard the tug.

Paul Stillwell: That saved you any problem of trying to find a place ashore then.

Mr. Hair: Yes.

Paul Stillwell: What did you do for liberty in the New York area?

Mr. Hair: Oh, we'd go to the city. I'd go to different USO places, things of that nature.† They had one on 137th Street there on Seventh Avenue in Harlem, which was terrific. They used to put on night shows. In fact, that's where I met my wife. At that time, she was a nurse up at Lincoln School, and the whole class came down. That's how I met my wife, was right there. That's when I was still an enlisted man. Then they had the big USO downtown. Occasionally, we would go down there.

Paul Stillwell: So things had opened up, as far as what you were able to go to.

---

* LCS – landing craft (support).
† USO – United Services Organization is a group of U.S. civilians who put on entertainment programs for service personnel and provide hospitality for them in many parts of the world.

Mr. Hair: Oh, yes. Yes, things had opened up in the city, and those were places you could go. There were still a lot of things that you had to be careful about that were still very much in operation. I remember I went down to the USO once, down there to a dance and entertainment, and this girl—this woman, I should say—came over to me and said she wanted to take some pictures of me. They said they were going to pay me for it, like $10.00 or something. I thought that was great. But then the catch in it was, she wanted me to pick 13 other guys, because she wanted a group of 14. So by that time, fellows were coming in from the South Pacific, and everybody was dark and whatnot, suntanned. So I wasn't sure of whom she wanted. So I just turned around to her and said, "Well, look, gee, I don't know whom you want here. You go ahead and pick it, but I'm available if you want to use me. I could use the $10.00."

So anyway, to make a long story short, she said, "Well, all right." So she went out and picked 13 white guys. So then I said, "This gal doesn't know that I'm black." So, anyway, they took us over to some building downtown there, around 42nd Street, and took our pictures. We were posing with these models, and I was the lead guy in this thing. She told me they were doing it for *Harper's Bazaar*; I think it was a cigarette advertisement. There was this beautiful blonde there holding this cigarette, and here was this sailor out there, making eyes at her and all that. But then after they took us in, they wanted to get our names, a little bit about our background, all that. They asked me, "Have you finished college?"

"Yeah, I finished Bethune-Cookman College."

"What is that?" So, anyway, I never saw that picture in *Harper's Bazaar*.

Paul Stillwell: Did you get your $10.00?

Mr. Hair: They paid me the $10.00.

Paul Stillwell: How did civilians treat you? I've heard stories about people buying drinks for sailors and treating them very courteously.

Mr. Hair: Oh, yes. I have a picture here, that just reminds me, of someone before your day, I'm sure, a gal named Oona May Carlisle. She was a black entertainer; she was a pianist and songstress. She invited me to a Joe Louis party on the roof up at the Theresa Hotel there at 125th Street and Seventh Avenue.* But they were very generous in that way, they really liked servicemen. She gave me this picture, which I have. But people were most generous about servicemen, they really were.

Paul Stillwell: There were some famous black nightclubs in Harlem. Did you go to those?

Mr. Hair: Oh, yes. Oh, yes. You had the Elks Club there, you had Small's Paradise, you had Lorraine's. There were many of them, a lot of after-hours spots. Of course, I didn't bother with those after-hour spots, and at that time, being an officer, if they caught you in one of those after-hours spots, there you go—a court-martial.

Paul Stillwell: You had to be holier than Caesar's wife.

Mr. Hair: That's right. That's right, we really had to.

Paul Stillwell: How did the trail start for you to become an officer? How did you get picked to be in that first group, do you think?

Mr. Hair: That's an interesting question. I really don't know to this day how I came to be picked. But I can tell you this, whether this has anything to do with it or not, I don't know, but when I was in Great Lakes, I'm pretty sure it was about the end of my boot camp training, or when I was in quartermaster school, I had to go over to the where Armstrong and all had their offices. I think I was assigned as color guard, and I had to go over there for something. While there, I happened to see the Navy newspaper that they

---

* Joseph Louis Barrow (1914-1981) was a black boxer who fought under the name Joe Louis. He won the boxing heavyweight title in 1936 and successfully defended the title 25 times before retiring in 1949. A later comeback failed. In June 1936, before becoming champion, Louis lost to German fighter Max Schmeling, then avenged that loss with a first-round knockout of Schmeling in June 1938.

had, and I looked through it. It said that the procurement office was advertising for more officers. I said, "What in the hell? I'll tear this out and see what's happening." So I did. I tore it out, put it in my pocket, while no officers were looking. So I went on back, and I filled the thing out, and I sent it in. I told them I was at Camp Robert Smalls, Great Lakes, Illinois, so there was no doubting about who I was. So whether that ever had anything to do with it or not, I don't know.

But with that, the first thing that I knew about it, in terms of my being into it, as I say, as I know it, I think Dennis Nelson and I were the only two to be a part of this school from some other place other than Hampton and Great Lakes.[*]

Paul Stillwell: Alves didn't come from those places either, did he?[†]

Mr. Hair: Oh, he didn't come from there either? I thought he was already at Great Lakes.

Paul Stillwell: Maybe he was.

Mr. Hair: That was my understanding, but maybe not. I'm pretty sure he was there, because, as I understand it, Alves had been around the camp.

Paul Stillwell: I see. He had come from a merchant background.

Mr. Hair: He had been in there, but after coming to the Navy, he went to Camp Robert Smalls. Now, that's the way I understand it, because he was going around telling the guys, "Man, don't you give no blood to no Red Cross," because the Red Cross discriminated. All that sort of stuff. He was quite militant at that time with the group. This is what I knew of him.

---

[*] Brigadier General Samuel Chapman Armstrong (1839-1893) was colonel of a black regiment in the Civil War. That led to his interest in vocational education for black students. In 1868 he founded the Hampton Normal and Agricultural Institute at Hampton, Virginia. His son, Daniel Armstrong, was the officer in charge of Camp Robert Smalls during World War II. Also during World War II the Navy set up a school on the campus of Hampton Institute and used it for training black sailors in specific occupational ratings.

[†] Although he went all the way through officer training with the Golden Thirteen, A. Alves was not commissioned at the end of the training period.

Mr. James E. Hair, Interview #1 (11/12/86) -- Page 54

Paul Stillwell: In what ways did the Red Cross discriminate?

Mr. Hair: Well, in those days, you see, the Red Cross would have blood, as I knew it then, but, say, if whites needed the blood, they're the ones who got it, not the blacks. It was something else, too, where they didn't want to give a white person any black blood. There were all kinds of prejudices that went on at that time. So Alves was really turned on about that thing. Anyway, I lost my point there.

Paul Stillwell: You were saying that most of the people came from Hampton or Great Lakes.

Mr. Hair: I was talking about how I came into it. So there I was, still aboard this tug. By the way, I think out of four and a half years that I was in the Navy, I think I was on the water like 40 months. But one day we were out—and I think this day we were out there doing something on those nets, out in those mines. We got this ship-to-shore call, saying, "Transfer James Hair to 90 Church Street immediately upon docking."

We came in, and I had my seabag and everything all ready. I went over to 90 Church Street.

Paul Stillwell: That was the headquarters for the Third Naval District.

Mr. Hair: That's right, in downtown Manhattan. So when I got there, I told them who I was. They looked at my identification and said, "Okay." They gave me this big brown envelope, something like this. On the back of it, in those days, they sealed them with this red wax, so you couldn't open that thing unless you broke the seal. But, anyway, they gave me these orders and told me to proceed immediately to Great Lakes, Illinois, and report to Commander Armstrong's office out there.

Paul Stillwell: Did you know why?

Mr. Hair: No, and they weren't about ready to tell me either. They didn't tell me a damn thing. So anyway, I said, "Yes, sir." They gave me a ticket to ride on. I said, "Oh, my goodness." I hadn't slept in a day and a night. I was exhausted. But lucky me, I went down to Penn Station to get the train, and I said, "I know what I'll do. I'm going to set my bags, I'm going to sit down right beside the gate here, because if the people start going in, I know I've got to hear them. Hopefully, if I drop off to sleep, somebody's going to wake me up," because I was dead tired. Sure enough, I went to sleep. You know, all those people left there and went and got on that train, and I didn't hear a one of them. I don't know what it was, but suddenly I woke up, and I looked down, and there was the train pulling out, and the porter was yelling, "All aboard!"

He had his stool and was moving out. I said, "Oh, my goodness! Look here!" I could see if I missed this, what was going to happen to me. But, anyway, I ran down there, and I yelled to the porter, "Let me on! Let me on!" And sure enough, he did. I threw my bags in, and I jumped on that train. I just made it.

I went to Chicago, and from there I went on out to Great Lakes. It must have been about 1:00 o'clock or so when I got there. I went over to Commander Armstrong's office, and I showed up with this envelope. They looked at me and said, "What are you doing here?"

I said, "Well, I came to see Commander Armstrong. I have some orders for Commander Armstrong." You can imagine the look they gave me. This Negro sailor coming in here at 1:00 o'clock in the morning, and he's got orders for Commander Armstrong? He must be an enemy or something. That was the reaction I got.

So, anyway, they had a conference. They went back there, and you could see them talking and pointing: "He says he's got some orders for the commander." So they came back there and asked me.

I said, "Yeah, here they are. I got these orders for Commander Armstrong." They looked, and they saw I had it right. So they took this on up.

Then they looked at me and said, "Well . . ."

I said, "I'm dead tired. Where can I get a little rest?"

They had no place for me. They didn't know I was coming, so they didn't have any place for me. So they went back and had another little conference and came out.

When they did, they said, "We'll tell you what. We'll take you to sick bay. This guy's got to be crazy."

So they took me down to sick bay. Apparently, this was the only place probably where they had an open bed or something like that. So I went down there, and I got in this bed. Just as I got in the bed, here came this corpsman around.* He said, "Hey, sailor, wake up. Take your APCs."†

Paul Stillwell: You were probably saying to yourself, "He thinks I'm sick."

Mr. Hair: Yes. I said to myself, "I know darn well there's only one way I can get out of this thing, is to go ahead and take these APCs." So I did. In another three hours, he came back, woke me up again. "Take some more."

I said, "Oh, no!" Son of a gun. But I would take them. I gulped them right down. "Yes, sir. Okay."

Paul Stillwell: It couldn't hurt.

Mr. Hair: Yes, that's right. Well, that was really something. Then I went on. Then the next day is when I went over to Armstrong's office, and then they sent me over to the other place, where I met the other guys for the first time. As I say, I possibly had seen Lear. I'm pretty sure I had seen him, but I didn't know him.

Paul Stillwell: Was this January of '44?

Mr. Hair: Was it January? It seemed like we started a little bit before January.

Paul Stillwell: Do you remember if Christmas had come yet?

---

* In World War II the enlisted medical specialists were pharmacist's mates, also known as hospital corpsmen.
† APC was the abbreviation for a commonly given analgesic tablet—aspirin, phenacetin, and caffeine. Its use has declined markedly because of its adverse side effects.

Mr. Hair: Christmas hadn't come, as far as I know.

Paul Stillwell: So it was late '43.

Mr. Hair: Late '43 sometime. I'm pretty sure it was before January that we got there. They put us in this barracks, and that's where the OCS was, right there in that barracks.[*] We spent the other several weeks that we were there in this class right in the barracks, except when we had to go out for swimming and stuff like that.

Paul Stillwell: What was the routine of a day in this officer training?

Mr. Hair: Well, first of all, we had classes. We had different instructors come in.

Paul Stillwell: Were they mostly naval officers?

Mr. Hair: Naval officers, yes. They were all naval officers, as I recall. They were all naval officers. Included in that group was Jack Dille.[†] You know, one of the other guys that was in there, too, I've forgotten now just how he took the group, but a few years ago, we had a letter from him that he'd seen the publicity about us, and told us that he is now living in Michigan, and that he certainly wished that if ever we were out there, we'd stop by to see him.[‡]

Paul Stillwell: He was one of the instructors?

Mr. Hair: Yes, one of the instructors.

---

[*] OCS – Officer Candidate School.
[†] Lieutenant (junior grade) John F. Dille Jr., USNR, was a battalion commander in the leadership structure at Camp Robert Smalls at Great Lakes in early 1944. See his recollections of the experience in Paul Stillwell's *The Golden Thirteen: Recollections of the First Black Naval Officers* (Annapolis: Naval Institute Press, 1993), pages 96-119.
[‡] In all likelihood, this is a reference to Lieutenant (junior grade) Paul D. Richmond, USNR, who set up the training curriculum for the black officer candidates. For his memories of the program, see *The Golden Thirteen*, pages 28-45.

Paul Stillwell: Did they do a good job of teaching you, do you think?

Mr. Hair: It varied. It varied, but, by and large, I would say that they did their job. There was at least one there, they admitted it later on, who came in under protest. But after he saw what we could do, he was really amazed, because he had never thought that a Negro could produce things, in terms of studies and things of that nature. He admitted it to us.

Paul Stillwell: I gather Dille was an exception in the other direction.

Mr. Hair: Dille just came to teach, and that was it. The military sent him there to teach, and that was what he was going to do. He was that kind of guy. The other guys, you could see some of them had some hang-ups. In a military setup, you carry out those orders. You may not carry them out to the highest, but you're going to carry them out.

Paul Stillwell: But you gather that Dille was putting his heart and soul into it.

Mr. Hair: He was. He was strictly military. He was there to teach, and that was it.

Paul Stillwell: How soon after you got there did you find out what you were there for?

Mr. Hair: Oh, the next day. The next day. Because, as I said, that night, after I got some sleep, the next morning I went right back to Armstrong, and that's when they told me.

Paul Stillwell: Did you get to see the orders, the ones that had been sealed up?

Mr. Hair: No. No. They had taken them back and opened them. Commander Armstrong opened them and just told me what it was.

Mr. James E. Hair, Interview #1 (11/12/86) -- Page 59

Paul Stillwell: What was the sort of word that was coming through Barnes's sister?* She was in Washington, I gather, and had some source of information. What kind of information were you getting from her?

Mr. Hair: I don't remember. I don't remember. But I remember there was some talk about that. I've forgotten now just exactly what it was about, something about some kind of information on what was happening, what was going to happen, those sort of things. Other than that, I don't remember.

Paul Stillwell: How long a day was it for you?

Mr. Hair: Oh, it was a long day. Day in and day out, right on through. We didn't leave that barracks, you see, except for going over to some of these swimming classes and lifesaving classes, stuff like that.

Paul Stillwell: Did you eat in the barracks?

Mr. Hair: No, no, that's right. I think we went across the street to eat someplace; we did go out to eat, because we had no facilities there for eating.

Paul Stillwell: But it really was just you 16.

Mr. Hair: The class, and that's where we stayed. There were 16 initially, but then, see, before the end of the class, some of them dropped out. They just like disappeared.

Paul Stillwell: Did the rest of you have any idea why the others were not making it?

---

* Phillip George Barnes and Samuel Edward Barnes were both members of the training class and subsequently of the Golden Thirteen. The oral history of Samuel Barnes is in the Naval Institute collection; Phillip Barnes died before he could be interviewed. The sister of Philip Barnes worked for the Navy Department in Washington, D.C., during World War II.

Mr. Hair: No, we didn't know then why it happened, but after that, there was a lot of scuttlebutt, as I mentioned, about Pinkney, that he falsified a record about the school he went to, or something like that.*

Paul Stillwell: Said he went to the University of Pennsylvania when he really hadn't.

Mr. Hair: Yes, that was the scuttlebutt that we got. Another guy that didn't make it, which Nelson, I think, pointed out in his study, was because he passed for white at one time.† This was an all-Negro thing. That's one thing about the Navy. In those days, if they said it was going to be one thing, it was that thing. So they said this was all Negro, so if you had passed at one time, then you didn't qualify. So that was one of the things brought out.

Paul Stillwell: Which one was that?

Mr. Hair: That was Alves.

Paul Stillwell: Theoretically, you had too. Why wasn't that counted against you?

Mr. Hair: What I mean by passing . . .

Paul Stillwell: He'd done it deliberately.

---

* J. B. Pinkney, A. Alves, and Lewis Reginald "Mummy" Williams were the three members of the 16 candidates who did not become officers. Bernard C. Nalty, *Strength for the Fight* (New York: The Free Press, 1986), makes the following statement on page 192: ". . . on January 1, 1944, sixteen black enlisted men entered a segregated officer candidate school at the Great Lakes Naval Training Station. Although all of them successfully completed the course, only twelve received commissions, a purely arbitrary number adopted by the Bureau of Personnel for reasons never explained. Of the remaining four, one became a warrant officer, and the others reverted to enlisted status."

† Nelson eventually retired from the Navy as a lieutenant commander. He died in 1979 before he could be interviewed as part of the Naval Institute's oral history program. Nelson's master's thesis was published by the Navy Department in 1948 and later came out as a book, *The Integration of the Negro into the U.S. Navy* (New York: Farrar, Strauss and Young, 1951).

Mr. James E. Hair, Interview #1 (11/12/86) – Page 61

Mr. Hair: See, for example, I don't know what it was, and I can't say, but what I mean by passing is that what they're looking at, not if you just go out to a restaurant or something like that without somebody knowing who you are, or something like that. I don't mean it in that sense. But I mean it in the sense that you're going to falsify your records.

Paul Stillwell: I see.

Mr. Hair: I don't know whether he did this or not. Say, for example, he was in the merchant marine. Did he go in there as white or black? I don't know.

Paul Stillwell: But that was the rumor.

Mr. Hair: Yes, that was just a rumor.

Paul Stillwell: What were the rumors about Pinkney?

Mr. Hair: About the school.

Paul Stillwell: Williams is the one.

Mr. Hair: Mummy? I don't know what happened to Mummy.* I can't remember. I don't remember what happened. I don't know. I know that he and Sylvester were very close.†

Paul Stillwell: As a matter of fact, Williams got White into the Navy, because he was at Great Lakes first.

---

* In an oral history interview, Lewis R. Williams indicated that he was told by Lieutenant (junior grade) Dille in 1944 that he would not be commissioned because an FBI investigation had turned up the fact that he had been a labor organizer for railroad station redcaps. In an interview subsequent to this one with Mr. Hair, Dille did not recall giving such an explanation to Williams.
† William Sylvester White, a good friend of Williams, successfully completed the training course and was commissioned.

Mr. Hair: Yes, right. Right.

Paul Stillwell: Judge White said he felt very bad that he had made it and Williams hadn't.

Mr. Hair: Yes, that's right. I know he did. He still holds some kind of sad feelings about that today.

Paul Stillwell: Understandably.

Mr. Hair: Occasionally, when we get around to talk, he'll bring it up again, about how bad he feels because Mummy didn't get in. I didn't know much about Mummy's background, because, you see, as I said, Dennis and I, at least speaking for myself, I didn't know this group until I got there, so I didn't know what had transpired with Sylvester and Mummy Williams and all like that until later on. After we had completed our courses and all that, I started getting information about that.

Paul Stillwell: I'm interested in your recollections of the individuals from that period, the ones who did make it. I'd just like to run through the list and see what springs to mind. What do you remember about Jesse Arbor, for example?* I might say for the benefit of the tape recorder, that you got a broad smile on your face when I mentioned his name.

Mr. Hair: Yes, that's right. Jesse is an outstanding guy. Where the guy gets all of his gift of personality from, I really don't know, but he is really some interesting person, very, very interesting. We've gotten into groups, and Jesse can carry us on for hours and hours in that group. He was really quite a guy, and he's always been that way too. He's always been that way. When we finished, when we graduated, Jesse—and I have a few pictures of it now—was the guy to invite us out to his home there in Chicago, and some

---

* Ensign Jesse Walter Arbor, USNR, was a member of the Golden Thirteen. His oral history is in the Naval Institute collection.

of his friends threw parties for us, and all that sort of thing. Jesse's always been that way ever since.

Paul Stillwell: How was he during the time you were studying?

Mr. Hair: Oh, very good, very cooperative. Very cooperative.

Paul Stillwell: I gather he was the guy that helped break the tension.

Mr. Hair: Yes, he did. He had quite a sense of humor, always a sense of humor.

Paul Stillwell: Did he tell jokes, or how was that manifested?

Mr. Hair: Jesse could take anything and see the humorous side in it. Say we were studying celestial navigation or whatever it might be. He could pick up some humor in that sort of thing. It was a great help to us during this time. He has always carried that right on through.

Paul Stillwell: Did you all feel like you were under a great deal of pressure during this training?

Mr. Hair: Oh, it was a lot of pressure. It was a lot of pressure. Not only that, but we were cooped in. We were there. Not only pressure to study, we knew we had to make it, see. As I say, and I can't speak for all the guys, but I think that one thing that sort of reflects those guys and all of us, what we had to go with through there, I think was the fact that—see, our goal in this class took precedence over all of Jim Crowism, racism, harassment.* We had to operate under control, as controlled individuals. We did, because we had all kinds of insults that would happen to us.

---

* Thomas D. Rice, a black minstrel singer, wrote a song and dance titled "Jim Crow" in 1832. Later in the century, the term took on the meaning of segregation of the races, as in "Jim Crow laws."

Paul Stillwell: During your training?

Mr. Hair: Well, yes, even sometimes during the training. We had to walk out. White guys, many white sailors and officers, to keep from saluting, they'd cross to the other side of the street. This would go on. You would get many insults, many insults. I remember when we were there in officer training, even when—to illustrate a little bit, we had to go over for a physical exam to the medical building, which was on the other side.

Paul Stillwell: Main side.[*]

Mr. Hair: On the main side. Right. We got there, and we had all these sailors, all white, and they came out and said, "All right, you boys, strip down. Everything off. Strip down." So we did. "Stand over there. Stand at attention." And we did. We went through all this sort of stuff. But then, without calling any names, it just so happened that one of the guys in the group had a pigmentation problem, and it so happened to be on his penis, which was half white and half black. But anyway, one of these guys spotted it. He went over and he got one of these 36-inch rulers, those old stick rulers. He came back, and he started hitting it, and he was banging it up. He was saying, "Hey, fellows, come here. Look at this! Look at this!" And banging this thing. In the meantime, this brother's sitting there, he's flinching with this thing, because, you know, that's a painful thing. "Look at this! Look at this!" So we were all standing at attention. I thought, "Oh, my God. This is the end right here. This is going to be the end." Any little thing, we could have blown it.

Paul Stillwell: Had you been warned against blowing up?

Mr. Hair: No. We knew that within ourselves. We knew that, if we were going to make it. That's why I say our goal took precedence over all these insults, racism and all. That was it. We knew that.

---

[*] The "main side" of the Great Lakes training station contained the administrative offices. It was separate from Camp Robert Smalls, the site of training for black sailors.

Paul Stillwell: You were going to have to be a little like your high school principal.

Mr. Hair: We were going to have to take it. Not out of fear, like the principal did, but we knew we had to take it if we were going to make it. But this went on and on, until finally he got a whole group, everybody came, everybody laughed and carrying on about it. "Here's this Negro here. Look at this, man, half white and half black." Banging his penis up and down. So I was standing there wondering how is this thing going to end. So, anyway, finally, the guy stopped, and he looked up at this fellow, and he said, "Hey, boy, where did you get this thing from?"

The fellow candidate there was a fellow brother; he said, "Well, you see, I was raised in a white neighborhood." I'm telling you, I said to myself, "Oh, my God! Are we going to make it out of here now?" But, I mean, there were innumerable things that went on.

Paul Stillwell: Did that defuse the tension?

Mr. Hair: It made them very angry. It made them very angry. They didn't know how to deal with it, so they went on back to their work, see. That thing really turned them on. They were hot. I guess they figured, too, if they started something, it was going to involve both of us. Under the military setup, I don't think they wanted that. Anything might have happened. The chances are that we would have been out.

Paul Stillwell: They would have been.

Mr. Hair: Yes, they probably would have been. May have, may not, we don't know. In those days, it was really rough. There were innumerable things that would go on like that, that would happen.

Paul Stillwell: We were talking about the individuals. What about Phillip Barnes? What do you remember of him?

Mr. Hair: Phillip was a wonderful guy from Washington, D.C., very wonderful guy, very pleasant, very helpful in the group. Of course, I could say that about all of us, because we were all very helpful there in the group that came to studying and all that. Very pleasant, very intelligent guy.

Paul Stillwell: I've gathered somewhat self-conscious about his weight, though.

Mr. Hair: I would imagine so, because he was kind of on the heavy side. I don't know why he was that way. But I understand he died shortly after.*

Paul Stillwell: I think so.

Mr. Hair: Shortly after the war sometime. I don't remember exactly. I must ask Sam Barnes about that. Evidently he had a problem with his weight, because he was quite chubby.

Paul Stillwell: What do you remember about Sam Barnes?

Mr. Hair: Sam. Sam was a terrific guy, same thing, very cooperative, very helpful, and in the group there, we would drill one another. You're good at navigation, you're good in Navy regs, Navy law, whatever you were grilled on, on many subjects, all of the guys were most giving in that direction. Very giving.

Paul Stillwell: Tutoring each other almost.

Mr. Hair: Oh, yes.

Paul Stillwell: I've gathered in personality he was almost the opposite of Arbor.

Mr. Hair: Oh, yes.

---

* Phillip Barnes died in March 1955 in Washington, D.C.

Paul Stillwell: Very quiet.

Mr. Hair: He was a quiet guy, a sharp sense of humor, but not as outgoing as Arbor. Sam was more reserved, I would say, than Arbor was.

Paul Stillwell: Was there any pecking order among the 16, or did you all treat each other as equals?

Mr. Hair: No, we treated each one as equals. We were all equal there. I guess in those days we had no choice. Sixteen guys all thrown into this one group there, and we were going to make it or not.

Paul Stillwell: There were differences. Some had been in the Navy longer, some had more education. But you threw that out the window.

Mr. Hair: Yes. In fact, now that you mention that, see, we didn't get into that really, as I can recall. I think it may have come up once or twice in terms of your educational background. For example, this thing that would come up, not in the sense of one having a little more than the other one had, anything of that nature, but to illustrate, I remember once Nelson was talking about the trouble that he had before he got in, which we were not aware of. The problem centered around the fact that his school had delayed in sending his transcript to the Navy, and they were holding it up because he hadn't paid his bill. Through that we learned what school he went to. I've forgotten now what school it was. But we didn't get into that at all. I can remember maybe one aspect where we knew that Sylvester was good in law, so when we would come to naval law and justice, a lot of times we would pick him up.

Paul Stillwell: That was an obvious choice.

Mr. Hair: Right. But what school he went to and so forth, we never really got into it. See, we didn't have time for that. You can imagine, study, study, study.

Paul Stillwell: I would think, though, that in one group, if you're together almost all the time, you've got to spend time chatting once in a while.

Mr. Hair: Oh, we would. We would chat just once in a while, but we didn't go into much like that. Most of the chatting then was strictly about Navy. For example, Navy dress, Navy code, all of that, how you've got to do this right, got to have your shoes shined right, all these sort of things we went into. I'm sure there probably were some other things, but we never got into talking about going on liberty, what you did last night on liberty, or any of those sorts of things. We didn't have any of that in those days.

Paul Stillwell: Did you have time to reflect then on the historic role that you were playing, being the first officers?

Mr. Hair: No, not as I recall, we didn't.

Paul Stillwell: Did you have a sense that if you failed, it could set things back, make it harder to have a Negro naval officer in the future?

Mr. Hair: I don't recall anyone there thinking in terms of failure. From my point of view, the entire group felt that we were here to do it, and we were going to do it, despite it, no matter what happened. We were going to do it, and we just had that determination. So I don't ever recall anyone talking about failure. I remember when we came up to about the end there, even then the talk was about, "When do we get our commission? Are they going to give it to us? If so, when?" It was that sort of thing. I don't remember any doubt there about were we going to make it or not.

Paul Stillwell: You must have talked about the disciplinary situation, at least. You were avoiding things that would hamper your chances.

Mr. Hair: Yes. Right, we did. We talked a lot about that. That's why I said that the shooting dice business, we had to straighten out right away.

Mr. James E. Hair, Interview #1 (11/12/86) – Page 69

Paul Stillwell: Right.

Mr. Hair: In those days, you see, it was presented in such a way that we had to be perfect specimens. We had to be that. Like a wooden soldier out there, we had to be perfect. That's the way we perceived it.

Paul Stillwell: What about Dalton Baugh?* What do you remember of him from that period?

Mr. Hair: He was right along there with the group. Dalton would go right along with the group. He was really a group man. He was really a group man.

Paul Stillwell: What special talent did he bring to it?

Mr. Hair: He was good. Dalton had had quite a background, as all of us, I think, in terms of education and whatnot. But I don't know whether he had been in education or what prior to that time. I can't remember. But as I say, he was quite a group man, and he really contributed his share to the group in our teaching and learning process. He was always a calm-headed person, very calm, never got excited about anything, very considerate. He's followed that right on throughout. Even after that, he was the same calm and considerate guy.

Paul Stillwell: What about George Cooper?†

Mr. Hair: George came from Hampton, and George was a part of the group—I'm trying to think now. George was a little bit different.

---

* Dalton Louis Baugh was a member of the Golden Thirteen. He died before he could be interviewed by the Naval Institute's oral history program.
† Ensign George Clinton Cooper, USNR, was a member of the Golden Thirteen. His oral history is in the Naval Institute collection.

Paul Stillwell: He had gotten a direct appointment as a chief petty officer. He hadn't gone through the boot camp training. He'd been teaching metalsmith work at Hampton.

Mr. Hair: Right. As I remember George in the group, George was more of a listener than a participant, unless you confronted him directly to get him to participate. But he was a good listener in the group. He was never the type to venture out, whether it was learning or whatever aspect or whatever we were doing. He was a good listener.

Paul Stillwell: I dare say when you did get something from him, it was pretty solid.

Mr. Hair: It was good, no doubt about it.

Paul Stillwell: He's a very profound individual.

Mr. Hair: Yes, he really is. He's a terrific guy, a terrific guy. I guess he's still that same way today. You mentioned about him getting involved. Practically every time we go, he says, "Look, fellows, I'm thinking of going into this or that." Occasionally he will send us some information on something that he had brought up to us, things of that nature, to get our thinking about it. But he's a real dynamic guy—no doubt about it.

Paul Stillwell: What else do you recall about Goodwin, other than his go-between role?

Mr. Hair: I think in the group, in addition, Goodwin kind of portrayed himself as the real intellectual of it. At one time, he had told me that he was Professor Einstein or Aristotle, or something like that.

Paul Stillwell: Did any of the rest of you resent this seeming "in" that he had with Armstrong?

Mr. Hair: How should I put it? I think that we recognized that this was something that Armstrong needed. He needed this go-between, and we didn't blame Goodwin for it, but

I guess at some time or another, we might have been a little apprehensive as to what he may have been telling him. So this is a natural curiosity sort of thing.

Paul Stillwell: Right.

Mr. Hair: Wondering what Goodwin was going to say, you know, because we knew Goodwin was all Armstrong, see. So in that sense, we were at times a little apprehensive.

Paul Stillwell: Was there a benefit to the group? Was he able to warn you about things or give you useful information from his meetings with Armstrong? Or was it mostly a one-way street?

Mr. Hair: I'm sure that some of the things that he mentioned were helpful to us. I can't think of anything specific right now, but I'm sure some of the things were.

Paul Stillwell: He helped you on that dice-throwing thing, if only to protect you from yourselves.

Mr. Hair: Yes, yes, yes. But I'm just thinking in terms of the stuff going back and forth from Armstrong. I mean, what he was giving to Armstrong and information he was bringing to us, in terms of what was happening. I'm sure that was most helpful to us.

Paul Stillwell: You don't recall any specifics on that?

Mr. Hair: No, I can't recall any specifics now. I can't.

Paul Stillwell: Did you get grades as you went along? Did you have a sense of how well you were doing?

Mr. Hair: Gee, it seemed like we did at one time, but it wasn't very often that we got any grades, if we did. I don't recall. I'm not sure whether we got grades or not.

Paul Stillwell: You must have had tests periodically.

Mr. Hair: We had many tests. We had plenty of tests. Maybe we got some grades; I don't remember. But we knew we were doing pretty well. We felt we were doing well.

Paul Stillwell: Goodwin may have been able to help you in that regard, give you some encouragement.

Mr. Hair: Right. Right. I don't remember the specifics about the grades now. I'm sure we may have gotten some.

Paul Stillwell: What about Charles Lear?* What do you recall of him?

Mr. Hair: Oh, he was a great guy, really a good Navy man. He followed the Navy law right to the letter. He was an outstanding individual and always ready and willing to help somebody else.

Paul Stillwell: And you've mentioned he was very devoted to his wife too.

Mr. Hair: Very devoted to her, he was. He was really a wonderful guy, a wonderful sailor. He had been in boot camp, and I think he had been an assistant to one of the company commanders or something like that before our class started. But Lear was a terrific guy, from Keokuk, Iowa. He was a great guy. I really admired that guy. As I said, we got to be very close friends there for the short time we were together.

Paul Stillwell: It must have been a shock to you when he died.

---

* Charles Byrd Lear was a member of the Golden Thirteen. Of the group he was the only one who became a warrant officer rather than an ensign. He died shortly after World War II.

Mr. Hair: And I didn't know about it until some years later. I didn't have any contact with any of the fellows, so I really lost all contact, except with one. John Reagan and I were together. But as I say, though, Charles Lear was just a wonderful sailor and wonderful officer. That's the type of guy that's not going to break any of the laws, no matter what the Navy says.

Paul Stillwell: A good citizen.

Mr. Hair: Oh, yes, he really was.

Paul Stillwell: Graham Martin.[*]

Mr. Hair: Oh, an outstanding guy. Graham and I were the only two to become skippers of some of the smaller craft.

Paul Stillwell: I think Frank Sublett had one too.

Mr. Hair: He did? I thought Sublett was with Graham.

Paul Stillwell: Yes. Sublett was the CO, and Martin was the XO.

Mr. Hair: Yes, that's right.

Paul Stillwell: Then Martin later got his own.

Mr. Hair: Yes. And Sublett later on got his own.

Paul Stillwell: Sublett was CO of one while Martin was XO, of the same boat.

---

[*] Graham Edward Martin is a member of the Golden Thirteen. His oral history is in the Naval Institute collection.

Mr. Hair: He was? Okay. I thought it was just the opposite. Maybe you're right.

Paul Stillwell: I think it was that way, because Sublett had had some seagoing experience before.

Mr. Hair: Okay. Good. But Graham was just an outstanding individual, still is today, a really great guy. He's another guy, man, I've never seen such devotion to a wife in all my days as that Graham.

Paul Stillwell: What qualities did he bring to your group while you were in training?

Mr. Hair: He was another one that fell right into the category of education. He was very educationally oriented, really contributed a lot in our group on different subject matters that would come up. Very open, very outgoing, a very giving type of individual in the group session.

Paul Stillwell: He made his life as a teacher, so that's understandable.

Mr. Hair: Yes, that's right.

Paul Stillwell: What about "Dennis the menace?"[*]

Mr. Hair: Dennis was something else, I'll tell you. We were all individuals, no doubt about it, but Dennis brought a new depth to the meaning of individuality. He was really something, and yet, going back, looking at those times, though, a lot of the things he did there were helpful to us, but it was very risky at the same time.

Paul Stillwell: Such as?

---

[*] This is a reference to Dennis D. Nelson II.

Mr. Hair: For example, I remember—I think this was right after we'd gotten our commission, and we were going out. We had our new dress uniforms on, wearing white scarves. Dennis came out with a red scarf, something like that. Dennis would do those things. We'd say, "Hey, you're not supposed to do that."

"Oh, heck." He was that way, and he was quite an adventurous guy. Of course, at that time, too, of course, we couldn't go to the officers' club or things like that. He took very much of a leadership role there in that aspect of it, for the right to go to the officers' club. Why should he be denied that? Someone there—I don't know if it was Armstrong or who it was, said we shouldn't go over there. I know it created a problem, but Nelson was ready to lead the group then, anytime we wanted to go. But a very dynamic individual. Nelson, too, now, as I understand it, was the only one who stayed in the Navy, but it took quite a lot of doing on his part to be able to stay in the Navy at that time. As I say, he was real fighter. He was the guy, too, that got us together eventually at the reunion, mainly because of Nelson, as I understand.

Paul Stillwell: How about John Reagan?[*]

Mr. Hair: When I went back to the Third Naval District after becoming an officer, then I was made skipper of this tug, it was really like a seven-day-a-week thing. I was the only skipper on board, had no relief. But occasionally they would give me like a weekend tied up or something like that. But, anyway, sometime after I was on there, then John came over and joined me on this tug. He was the executive officer. So we got together. At the time, he was learning how to operate a boat, things of that nature, so we stayed together for a few months, until I went aboard the USS *Mason*.[†] Prior to that he didn't know how to handle a boat or anything of that nature.

Paul Stillwell: He didn't have the experience you did.

---

[*] Ensign John Walter Reagan, USNR, was a member of the Golden Thirteen. His oral history is in the Naval Institute collection.
[†] In 1945 Hair became the first black officer in the destroyer escort *Mason* (DE-529), a ship with an all-black enlisted crew.

Mr. Hair: No, he didn't have the experience at that time. But anyway, as I said, we were together for a few months. Then after that, I had the experience with the captain of the *Mason*, and I went aboard the USS *Mason*. Then I didn't see John anymore then. He went one way and I went another way at that time, because he did become skipper of the tug. He went someplace after that.

But I did see him again. I ran across John. In 1950 I was graduated, and I got this call from John in the city. He came to my graduation, and that was the first time I had seen him. Then shortly after that, he went away again, but he had gone back in the Navy. Then I lost track of him again; I didn't know where he had gone. I think he went to the Korean War or something like that. I believe he did. I think he did.

Paul Stillwell: What did you graduate from in 1950?

Mr. Hair: Fordham University. I went there to the School of Social Services. Then, after that, up to the New York School of Social Services for advanced courses toward a doctorate. I never got a doctorate degree, though. You couldn't matriculate to a doctorate then. You had to be director of an agency for 15 years or something like that before you had the necessary requirements.

But anyway, then after that I went to the *Mason*.

Paul Stillwell: I wanted to finish up this run through the list. Frank Sublett.[*]

Mr. Hair: Frank was another good person to the group. He was very giving and very helpful in the group. He contributed to all of our studies. He was a very good guy, but he was somewhat on the quiet side in terms of the group. That's why I'm hesitating to try to get a picture.

Paul Stillwell: He was also the youngest and may have been a little awed by the rest of you.

---

[*] Frank Ellis Sublett, Jr., was a member of the Golden Thirteen. His oral history is in the Naval Institute collection.

Mr. Hair: Yes, probably was. Probably was. He just sort of took a back seat, but yet was a part of the group, because he was learning and contributing all the time. He wasn't as active as some of the other guys who were there.

Paul Stillwell: Who would you say were the most active?

Mr. Hair: I'd say Martin was very active, Dennis Nelson was very active. A few guys there were very active. Many times Goodwin would be very active. Depending on the subject that we were discussing—it was something in math, Goodwin would be or Graham, the type of guys that would come through. Navigation and all that sort of stuff, they used to refer to me as the "old salt" for dead reckoning and stuff. He really, as I say, he was not openly active, a little bit reticent in the group. I'm talking about Sublett, but really, still, very much a part of it.

Paul Stillwell: What about Syl White?

Mr. Hair: Sylvester White. Oh, yes, he was very active, too. In fact, we used him a lot when we came to naval law and justice, those courses. We'd use Syl quite a bit. He was quite giving. I got to know him quite well, too. He was really something.

Paul Stillwell: After you had gone through this period of training, I don't know if they called you 90-day wonders, but, in any event, you were commissioned.[*] What kind of a feeling did you have when you finally got that new uniform?

Mr. Hair: It was a great feeling, and it was a mixed feeling also. Probably some mixed feeling there, because we knew we had accomplished this, simply being the first black line officers in the Navy. At the same time, we knew that just by getting this commission, we were aware of the fact that this wasn't the end of it. There was a big job ahead of us now that we had to do. We were now officers in the Navy, and this was a

---

[*] The members of the Golden Thirteen were commissioned in March 1944.

step in the direction of breaking down the all-white-officer Navy. We were thrown out there, as the examples now that we were officers, and we had to be the leaders now.

Paul Stillwell: Did you feel that you would get much more scrutiny than a white ensign, let's say?

Mr. Hair: Oh, no doubt about that. Oh, no doubt about it. We would. I mean, oftentimes you were seen almost as a spectacle coming down the street. "Oh, my goodness, look at there." I guess some of these things were to be expected, with the situation being what it was at that time. Oh, yes.

Paul Stillwell: I know that all of you had been investigated pretty thoroughly. Did you get the feeling that the people who were picked for this training would be ones who would react well to that pressure?*

Mr. Hair: Oh, yes. I think we had a very dynamic group of individuals here, and a strong group of individuals who we had demonstrated all of this ability for self-control, to withstand all of the harassment and insults and things, even while in school. Of course, being segregated there in this building, separated away from the other schools, that would be normal under normal conditions. So you had a bunch of guys there who could go through that and come out. That, in itself, demonstrated a lot of strength.

Paul Stillwell: Had their investigation of you turned up the business about your brother-in-law being killed and your reaction?

Mr. Hair: No. I'm sure it hadn't.

Paul Stillwell: George Cooper said it was so thorough in his case that they knew about a fight he'd had when he was eight years old.

---

* The FBI had investigated the potential officer candidates before the selection was made of the 16 who would undergo the training course in early 1944.

Mr. Hair: I don't think they had in my case. I don't think they had. I think one of the reasons for it, see, this was a brother-in-law that didn't have the same name as I did. That might have stopped it had they known about it. As I say, this was a brother-in-law. Plus, I think, one of the other factors that would militate against them even finding out about it at that time was the fact that I had such a wonderful record. The way I felt about it then, no matter who they went to, whether it was Arlie Peacock and Mildred Peacock, or James Stuckey, the chauffeur I told you about, or any college president, or Mrs. Bethune. They all gave me terrific recommendations. In fact, I have a letter now from Mrs. Bethune.

Paul Stillwell: I'm sure that would count for a lot.

Mr. Hair: You know what I mean? So with this sort of thing, I don't think they would have had any questions about looking to see if there was anything devious in this guy's life. No, I don't think they'd have been able to touch that one, when they saw all these good recommendations about me from both white and black. This is just my thinking on it. I doubt if they looked into that aspect.

Paul Stillwell: Did you have any choice of duty, where you would go, once you were commissioned?

Mr. Hair: No. See, I was already assigned to the Third Naval District.

Paul Stillwell: So that just resumed?

Mr. Hair: Yes.

Paul Stillwell: Obviously you wouldn't go back to the same job as quartermaster on board the *Penobscot*.

Mr. Hair: No, that's true. But when I reported back, that's when they made me skipper of a tug then.

Paul Stillwell: What was the name of that one?

Mr. Hair: That was the *YTB-215*, electrical reciprocating job, which was beautiful. Whereas the old *Penobscot* was one of those old steam reciprocating jobs, oh, my God, that was most dangerous, working out there with those things around those mines, because a lot of times the man down in the engine room couldn't hear. We had this bell system. He'd think he heard one bell or two bells. It was really tough on that thing. I went back aboard that.

Paul Stillwell: Did that boat have many of the same types of duties that *Penobscot* had?

Mr. Hair: Same thing. A lot of towing, a lot of assisting of ships, docking. It was hard. I remember once during the severe winters, when the ships had to get up the Hudson to get ammunition. We had an ammunition dump up the Hudson, near West Point. We had to put icebreakers on that thing and go ahead and serve as an icebreaker for the ships to get through. So we had all kinds of jobs there.

I never will forget one night, though. We got this call to go out to assist a ship. We were having a hurricane. Oh, gee. We got this call, "Proceed immediately to help this ship in distress at such and such a point." Water was standing up over the whole boat. You couldn't see 5 feet in front of you. Water, just tons of it, coming. We got this order to go out to assist this ship, and I took off and gave orders for us to get under way, and we started out. But if there was any time I thought we were really going to go under, it was that night. I never will forget.

I had this guy aboard ship there, everybody called him Shorty. Shorty had quite a sense of humor, but Shorty wasn't trying to be funny this time. He came up in the pilothouse just as we started out, and he had on ten life jackets. Ten life jackets. Right away, I turned and I looked at him, and I started cursing. I said, "What in the hell are you doing in here? What kind of damn sailor are you? Get those damn jackets off! Get 'em off!" And he ripped them off like mad. But, oh, what that did for the crew! Oh, boy, here was this brave skipper. "If he's not afraid, why should we be afraid?" It was that sort of attitude. But I'll tell you, after Shorty walked away, I said to myself, "Damn, I'd like to pick up those life jackets and put them on myself." That was some time, though.

Paul Stillwell: Did you have an all-black crew?

Mr. Hair: No, it was an integrated crew.

Paul Stillwell: Does that make you the first black officer to have whites working for him?

Mr. Hair: I don't know.

Paul Stillwell: Sure got to be one of the first.

Mr. Hair: Yes. I don't know, because what about Graham and Sublett?

Paul Stillwell: I don't recall.

Mr. Hair: I don't know exactly when they became skippers, but I know as soon as I came back, see, I went right aboard there as skipper, and I don't know when they were assigned or shipped out. I may have been.

Paul Stillwell: Did the crews take orders without any problems?

Mr. Hair: Oh, yes, no problems. I was fortunate, too. I had a heck of a good group. I had a boatswain there who had been on sailing ships once with the Swedish Navy or one of them. That guy could run up a mast pole like a monkey, right up there. He taught the crew, he really did. The other thing I was fortunate in was I got a cook by the name of Blake. Blake had cooked for admirals at one time, so you know he had to be good, to work up to being a cook for an admiral. The only reason why I got him was because of his age. Blake didn't want to get out of the service, the war was going on, one of those patriotic guys. So they decided to assign him to some of the smaller craft instead of to a battleship or destroyer because of his age. Oh, could that guy cook! Our big problem was with our stores, which he was in charge of. We ate the best of foods and everything. But we were underdrawn something like $2,000 on our stores from the commissary, where we got all our food. That was simply because of Blake.

Paul Stillwell: He had the experience and knew how to do it.

Mr. Hair: He knew how to do it; he really did. We had two cooks, and the other guy was a lousy cook. Fortunately, Blake saved him.

Paul Stillwell: Did you have any disciplinary problems in the crew?

Mr. Hair: Oh, yes, one time. Once I had a disciplinary problem. What it was, the boats had ordered the electrician to fix the light up on the mast after it broke; the light was out. Actually, the guy forgot about it. Well, hell, in the service, you don't forget. So we started out that night and I had no light up there. In towing, you have to have so many lights up, whether it's astern or at the side.

Paul Stillwell: The rules of the road.

Mr. Hair: That's right. Well, we didn't have this light. We didn't realize that until we started out. So, anyway, I had to do something to him, because this was against the rules. I gave him the punishment of shining up about 15 buckets with steel wool. That was the old thing in the Navy.

Paul Stillwell: Extra duty.

Mr. Hair: Polish the buckets, which he did gladly. That was the only thing I ever had.

Paul Stillwell: I'm sure that having a skipper who knew his business meant a lot as far as the leadership of the crew.

Mr. Hair: Oh, yes.

Paul Stillwell: If they respect you professionally, they respect you as a person.

Mr. Hair: Oh, yes, they did. They really did.

Paul Stillwell: I gather that morale was pretty good, from what you say.

Mr. Hair: Yes.

Paul Stillwell: The meals certainly are a big part of that.

Mr. Hair: Oh, yes. Yes, that's true.

Paul Stillwell: Did you get pretty good liberty for the crew?

Mr. Hair: Yes, it was pretty good. Pretty good. We got something like 24 hours every other week or something like that. Occasionally we could give 72 hours, depending on the situation. But that was unusual, to get 72 hours.

Paul Stillwell: What was the farthest that the boat got away from New York Harbor?

Mr. Hair: Down the Atlantic coast, just down off of that light down there. We used to go out and down the Atlantic coast.

Paul Stillwell: Cape May?

Mr. Hair: Almost to Cape May; not quite to Cape May. Down there and then over to Connecticut. Then, of course, all in and around New York, in the Hudson, icebreaking, and something like that.

Paul Stillwell: But it was essentially a yard tug rather than oceangoing.

Mr. Hair: Yes, a yard tug. We'd work out around Ambrose Channel and around out there—the nets and things of that nature.

Paul Stillwell: I imagine that was a feeling of great satisfaction to have your own boat.

Mr. Hair: Oh, yes, it really was. It really was. In fact, when I went aboard the *Mason*, I sort of hated to give it up.

Paul Stillwell: One thing led into another, that the skipper of the *Mason* was very impressed by both the appearance and performance of your tugboat.[*] So how did that lead into the transfer?

Mr. Hair: Well, as I understand it, he was impressed with that, and he just requested, through Washington, the Bureau of Naval Personnel, to have me transferred. He had some connections down there with someone. The way he got on the *Mason* was through someone he knew down there in Personnel. So when he wanted me aboard there, he just contacted the person down there, and I got my orders to go aboard the USS *Mason*.

Paul Stillwell: Along with the disappointment over losing your boat, though, now you were getting to a bigger and more capable vessel.

Mr. Hair: Yes. Right.

---

[*] The commanding officer of the destroyer escort *Mason* at that point was Lieutenant Commander Norman H. Meyer, USNR. For Meyer's description of his command of the ship and relationship with Hair, see *The Golden Thirteen*, pages 192-213.

Paul Stillwell: And one that has a combatant role.

Mr. Hair: Yes, which is something that I had looked forward to. I think this was the same with a lot of the other guys. They were hoping they would get on some man-of-war or something of that nature.

Paul Stillwell: You were the first to do that.

Mr. Hair: Yes.

Paul Stillwell: What kind of job did you have on board the *Mason*?

Mr. Hair: I was first lieutenant, in charge of all the deck operations.

Paul Stillwell: What specific operations do you remember?

Mr. Hair: Well, seeing that all deck . . .

Paul Stillwell: She had some depth charge tests. Were you on board for that?

Mr. Hair: Yes, I was on there for that. I had to see that all those things were working in good order. Everything had to be right, because that was my responsibility. So I was the one who answered to the captain, even if the anchor didn't work right, depth charges, and things like that. I was not the gunnery officer to take care of the guns or anything of that nature, but all these other things.

Paul Stillwell: But deck area, per se.

Mr. Hair: Boats and all that on board. Everything had to be shipshape, all your hatches, portholes, everything else pertaining to the ship.

Paul Stillwell: How capable would you say the enlisted crew was on board the *Mason*?

Mr. Hair: It was very good, very good, a quite capable crew. They were really good. I'll never forget, we went into Bermuda there once and had a dress-down. Everything was just spic and span when we went in there. We got some pictures.

Paul Stillwell: Justice White said he thought that the *Mason* had been somewhat shortchanged, because skippers would not send their best people away; they'd want to keep them for themselves and send lesser quality people. But your experience didn't bear that out, I take it.

Mr. Hair: No. In fact, this one guy that I know about from the *Mason* was the electrician aboard the ship. So we had a wonderful crew. But the thing is with the *Mason*, it was different then than the smaller boats, like the tugboats. On the tugboat, everybody got to be very close. You knew everyone, and it was an integrated crew. Here on the *Mason* it was a much larger crew, and you didn't have that closeness there, although you had some of that where the guys really got to know one another. But in terms of their job operation, they did a real good job, I thought. It was really quite good.

Paul Stillwell: I take it you were impressed by the skipper. You recounted to me something before the tape started about your first meeting with him. If you could repeat that, please.

Mr. Hair: Oh, yes. That was interesting, because after seeing me down there around Sandy Hook, New Jersey, where a lot of destroyers were in there at anchor, he called me aboard to have lunch with him, which was rather unusual in those days. Senior officers didn't call junior officers up to have lunch with them, especially a black officer at that time. So imagine what this did to my crew. You could see all the question marks all over their heads, wondering what was happening. "Look at our skipper."

But, anyway, I went aboard, and he greeted me there. At that time, he was carrying a copy of Dr. Myrdal's book under his arm, *An American Dilemma*.* He was very candid, and he told me that he had observed my tugboat out there, he was impressed with it, and he wanted me to come aboard, because this was a new assignment for him, and he didn't know anything about blacks. He wondered if he could talk to me about it. So I said, "Yes, sure, I'll be glad to talk." We got in and started talking about different things about blacks. I don't remember all the specific things, but we covered the black problem in America, some of the things that had come from Dr. Myrdal's book, and so forth.

I guess, in a way, I was reassuring him that, "As long as you're capable of doing a job, go ahead, you can do it. You don't have anything to worry about." Because what was noticeable about him at that time was he showed no signs of any prejudices whatsoever. He was a guy who was completely open, and all of a sudden, he was in this position in which he didn't know anything about the cultural aspects of his crew, or anything of that nature, but he was eager to learn something about it. It was that sort of thing. So we had a very pleasant discussion, I guess for half an hour, 45 minutes—something like that.

Then after that, we left. It was a very pleasant thing. After I left, a couple of days after that, I got my orders to go aboard the *Mason*, which was really a step upward, although I hated to leave the crew and all on the tug. I'm sure they felt the same thing with me. They were really disheartened at that time because I was leaving. I said, "Look, this is a part of military life, and we have to move on." So they understood that.

Paul Stillwell: The war was really winding down at that point.

Mr. Hair: Yes, that's right.

Paul Stillwell: The war in Europe was over. Was there some thought that the *Mason* would go over to the Pacific?

---

* Swedish economist Gunnar Myrdal did a study titled *An American Dilemma: The Negro Problem and Modern Democracy*, funded by the Carnegie Foundation and published in 1944. It subsequently came out in revised editions and had an influential role in U.S. racial relations.

Mr. Hair: Yes, there was some thinking about that, that it might go to the Pacific. But as the war was grinding down in Europe, we got these orders then to decommission the *Mason* down in Charleston, South Carolina.[*]

Paul Stillwell: The captain, when he took you down South, was also using you to integrate an officers' club down there.

Mr. Hair: Oh, yes, right, right. I remember that. And you know what? The captain got a lot of heat about that, but the interesting thing about it, at that time, another black officer had come aboard the USS *Mason*. He was Ensign McIntosh.[†] What actually happened then was McIntosh and I were going out for dinner that night, and we were going to find someplace there around Charleston to have dinner. As we were going over the gangplank, Captain Meyer then looked out at us and yelled, "Hey! Hair and McIntosh! Where you going?"

So we said, "We're going to dinner."

So he said, "Well, wait for me. I want to go. Wait for me. I want to go with you."

We said, "Okay." At that time, we hadn't discussed where we were going or anything. So he came on out, and we went on over to the officers' club. But he was the one that got the heat for it, you know. All the white officers were blaming him for bringing these Negroes over there for dinner, and that wasn't the situation at all.

Paul Stillwell: He said that you felt uncomfortable going there.[‡]

Mr. Hair: Uncomfortable?

Paul Stillwell: Is that the way you remember it?

---

[*] The decommissioning was on 12 October 1945, the month after the Japanese surrendered.
[†] Ensign John McIntosh, USNR.
[‡] Shortly before this interview with James Hair, Commander Meyer had done an interview that provided his recollections of their service together.

Mr. Hair: Oh, surely. Surely. Surely.

Paul Stillwell: That's not where you might have gone anyway if you hadn't been with him then?

Mr. Hair: No, no, no. We were going over there anyway. McIntosh and I were going to the officers' club, but what I mean by being uncomfortable, when you go into a situation like that, where you cannot be at ease, then it's uncomfortable. But we were determined we were going to do it. That's what I mean by being uncomfortable, and we were. There's no doubt about it.

Paul Stillwell: You would have been uncomfortable whether you had been with him or by yourselves.

Mr. Hair: Oh, yes, oh, yes, no doubt about it.

Paul Stillwell: But, in effect, he protected you from getting direct heat.

Mr. Hair: Yes. Right. And then, on the other hand, knowing the situation, I guess I may have been a little bit more uncomfortable by him being there, because I knew what the situation was, and I realized that right away they were going to accuse him, whereas that wasn't necessarily the case, because we were going to go anyway.

Paul Stillwell: Was there any discussion about you avoiding going on liberty with the black enlisted men in the crew?

Mr. Hair: No, but that's just something you didn't do in the Navy in those days. That wasn't protocol. You didn't do that. You just didn't associate with the sailor on liberty or anything. You didn't do it.

Paul Stillwell: Admiral Gravely did once and got in trouble for it.*

Mr. Hair: Yes, right. But that was against regs in those days, you see, and we didn't do it. However, I know this, though. I never will forget once when we were here in New York, and the crew, it was around Christmastime.

Paul Stillwell: Which ship were you in at the time?

Mr. Hair: I was still skipper of this tug.

Paul Stillwell: That would have been late 1944, then.

Mr. Hair: Yes, but it was something that was happening. I'm trying to think of what it was. I can't remember what it was, but some of the black crew were from Harlem. One of them was having a party for the entire crew, up at his place. So they invited us, the officers. So anyway, I asked them about it, where it was going to be, so forth and so on, but I told them, "Look, I can't come to the party, because it's against Navy regs, but I'd like to contribute to it."

They said this was okay with them. I said, "Fine. Look, I'll bring a couple of hams," because we had all these stores. We were like $2,000 underdrawn. Anyway, so John Reagan and I at that time, each one of us went and got a ham. At that time, as an officer, you could walk right out with a bag, and they didn't question you. So we left. They had gate sentries there.

Paul Stillwell: This was from the commissary?

Mr. Hair: Yes, this is where we docked over at Staten Island. They had these gates there that when you leave on liberty, you had to go through them, all officers and enlisted men.

---

* See the Naval Institute oral history of Vice Admiral Samuel L. Gravely Jr., USN (Ret.). In 1971 he became the U.S. Navy's first black admiral. Long before that, when he was an ensign in 1945, he was arrested by military policemen in Miami for impersonating an officer. His commanding officer was able to defuse the situation.

If the enlisted man had a bag, they'd search it, but they wouldn't do that to an officer, which we knew. So anyway, each one of us got a ham. We didn't tell them where we got it, but we got it in the stores. We each got a ham. We got the address, and we went on up by the place where this sailor was from, met his family and all that, and told him, "Here's the hams we wanted to contribute." Wished them the best: "Have a grand time," and all that, but we left. I'm just saying this, since we did not participate in their social activities.

Paul Stillwell: In that case, it might have been permissible. If it was an all-ship's event, officers could go to that. But you obviously were being very careful.

Mr. Hair: Yes, that's right. Then, you see, one of the sailors lived there, and he was having it at his house, which was a different thing. It might have been different had it been at some neutral place.

Paul Stillwell: That's true, yes.

Mr. Hair: We didn't get involved with that, no.

Paul Stillwell: Was the exec in the *Mason* as open-minded and helpful as the captain?

Mr. Hair: Oh, yes. We had a guy, Phillips, from Philadelphia.* Phillips was quite open, very helpful, a real dedicated, patriotic guy. I always found him to be very, very helpful.

Paul Stillwell: Did you stand deck watches in that ship?

Mr. Hair: At times, yes.

---

* Lieutenant John Phillips, USNR. As Commander Meyer recalled in his interview, he had gotten rid of two subordinate officers who were not comfortable serving in a ship with a black crew. Phillips did support Meyer's efforts, so he was moved up to the role of executive officer.

Paul Stillwell: That was a step up professionally for you. Were you disappointed when she got decommissioned?

Mr. Hair: Oh, yes. I really hated to leave that ship. You'd be on these ships for a while and become attached to them. I hated to really leave that ship. But yet, at the same time, I recognized this was a part of military life. You get your orders, and you just have to go. So that's the way I accepted it.

Paul Stillwell: Did you have a hand in the mothballing process?

Mr. Hair: No, no. We just had to take it in the dock. After that, I had my orders to leave and go to the Pacific.

Paul Stillwell: Where did you go from there?

Mr. Hair: From there, I was assigned then to go to the Pacific to join the Seventh Fleet. En route to the Pacific, I had to go to the Naval School of Law and Justice at Port Hueneme, California. That's right near Oxnard. So I stopped by there and took that course, which then qualified me to serve as counsel in the Navy on any court-martial case. It was a very democratic sort of court. The sailor would choose whichever counsel he wanted to represent him in different cases aboard ship. So anyway, I completed that course. There again, I was the only black guy in that course, but how many of those fellows knew that I was black, I don't know.

After completing that, I went on up to San Francisco and caught a troopship going to Shanghai. Oh, my goodness, that was really, really something. I got this guy from Iowa or someplace out there. I've forgotten his name. I've sort of tried to block that out. But, oh, he hated Negro officers. I was the only black officer aboard the ship. We must have had about 1,000 guys on there, you know, sailors, officers. And out of this, one black officer and maybe 30 black sailors on this ship. A big crew, huge. But every place I would go, there was this guy. Oh, "nigger" this, "nigger" that, "nigger" so and so. Oh, he was horrible. Sometimes I'd just duck him to get around and go some other place.

Paul Stillwell: Was this an enlisted man?

Mr. Hair: No, he was an officer. He was an officer, but one of these guys that was looking for trouble. You knew he was looking for trouble. So I was just trying to circumvent him the best way I could. The situation was very tense. So we kept going out there.

I never will forget, on these troop transport ships, they always had a lot of activity, a lot of physical activity—boxing and all that. We had this black guy who obviously had had a background in boxing, because he was just taking everybody out. So this went on every day. No matter who'd get in there, he'd knock him out. He must have had a lot of professional training, because he was terrific. These guys keep coming up. They were going to beat this damn nigger. "Come on, we're going to beat this nigger." Every time, he'd knock them out. So this was creating more and more tension.

One day, I was in the officers' room, and who walked in? This guy didn't recognize me sitting over there in the corner. It was the chaplain, but he had a special project. He said, "Look, we've got to find some of these white boys who can beat that damn nigger." This was his main project, to find white boys to beat this nigger. And here I was, right in there. Then, to top it off, one of the brothers there, one of the black sailors there, started playing dice, shooting dice for money. This guy was taking everybody right and left; he was a shark. His hands were quicker than his eyes, you know, and he could just rake it in. Well, these guys get mad. Then the next thing, they started getting these guys together, and they were going to get all these niggers and throw them overboard, that sort of thing. Then it came up into the officers' ranks. Some of them were saying to get rid of them, throw them overboard. "Who's going to miss them?" It was that sort of thing.

One night, there in the officers' quarters, it got really tense. They were talking about what they were going to do. This time I started really worrying, because I was the only one there, and what the hell was going to happen, with all this stuff going on and the tension that existed there? So, anyway, fortunately, there was this white officer there, I'll never forget, a guy named Pierce, and he stood up and spoke. The gist of his speech was, "Let's don't be ignorant and stupid." I don't know where that guy went after that, because we separated, one way or the other. Of course, I didn't do anything that would exacerbate his position. I didn't try to be friendly with him. But this was the sort of thing that went on throughout that trip.

Paul Stillwell: Do you remember which ship that was?

Mr. Hair: I don't remember the name of that ship. It was some troopship. Every day on this ship, they'd give you the news reports about the leading news stories. We had this news announcer come on every day. "Now hear this. Now hear this." And today I believe it was John Cameron Swayze who was our news announcer.[*] His voice was just like him. I never got to meet him on the ship to know if that was him, but it sounded just like John Cameron Swayze. I don't know if he was in the Navy or not, but he certainly sounded like John Cameron Swayze. After all these tense situations going on, then he comes on reporting the news, and the main lead story that day was, he said, "Now hear this. Now hear this. The main news today is that Father Divine just married one of his white angels."[†] You remember Father Divine?

Paul Stillwell: Well, I've heard about him.

Mr. Hair: He was this religious type of person. So imagine all the people started getting red. Everybody was getting mad. Fortunately, John Cameron went on to say, "But although he married one of his white blonde angels, we should know that Father Divine never sleeps with any of his angels." Oh, well, that's okay then. The things we had out there, it was unbelievable.

Paul Stillwell: So you finally got out to China?

---

[*] Swayze was a network newsman, first on radio and then on television.
[†] George Baker Jr., also known as "Father Divine," was a black spiritual leader from the early part of the 20th century until his death in 1965. He founded the International Peace Mission movement. After his first wife, Peninniah died in 1943, Divine married a Canadian white woman named Edna Rose Ritchings in April 1946.

Mr. Hair: Yes, made it to China. Then I said, "Oh, my goodness. This is great. Now I can get this guy off my back." So I went to headquarters there, got my orders to go on board the *LST-1026*.* When I got there, they told me the LST had just gone down to Hong Kong and told me to catch a destroyer which was just getting ready to pull out for Hong Kong. So I dashed over there and got on this destroyer to go down to Hong Kong. I thought, "Thank God, I got rid of this guy that's been on my back with 'nigger this' and 'nigger that.'" When I got on this destroyer, they showed me where I was to stay.

I walked in, and this guy said, "Hi, nigger." It was this same guy. He had to go down to Hong Kong and catch his ship too.

I said, "Lord, no!" But, anyway, we went on down there and finally got to Hong Kong, and I got my LST, and that's where I left him. I don't know where he went. He was assigned to some other ship.

Paul Stillwell: What was your job in the LST?

Mr. Hair: Deck officer. At that time, V-J Day had just ended.† So we were doing a lot of work in support of Chiang Kai-shek, to keep the Communists from coming in.‡

Paul Stillwell: You were probably a jaygee by then, weren't you?

Mr. Hair: Yes, I was a jaygee.§ First it was like training them, taking them out on cruises for ship handling, showing them how to operate LSTs and things of that nature. I'm getting ahead of myself, because when I first got on, we were still carrying tanks. Because those big LSTs would carry 33 tanks. Shortly thereafter, we went right in to help Chiang Kai-shek, training his forces and whatnot. Then, in addition to that, then we

---

* USS *LST-1026*, a tank landing ship, was commissioned 7 June 1944. She displaced 1,625 tons, was 328 feet long, 50 feet in the beam, had a maximum draft of 11¼ feet, and a top speed of 11.6 knots. After World War II service in the Philippines she operated in the China area until mid-1946 and was decommissioned 11 August 1946.
† V-J Day—Victory over Japan Day, marked the end of the war in the Pacific on 15 August 1945. Because of the time difference it was 14 August in the United States when combat ended.
‡ Generalissimo Chiang Kai-shek served as President of Nationalist China on the mainland from 1943 to 1949 and as President of the Republic of China on Taiwan from 1950 until his death in 1975.
§ Jaygee – lieutenant (junior grade).

got into helping him by transporting his armies around. He had one army in French Indochina, I think. We went down there and picked up that, his A-number-one crack army. There was another one right around Hong Kong that we got. Then one we took up through the Gulf of Pohai to Chefoo, China.

Then after that, then we took the other one from Haiphong, French Indochina, up to [unclear], Manchuria. The war was still going on there between the Japanese, the Chinese, and whatever. You could hardly tell who was shooting at whom. The same thing down in French Indochina. It was rough. They had pillboxes on every corner. You didn't know who was on which corner, which group on which corner. You couldn't walk on the sidewalk if you went in. You had to get right in the center of the street, because they could grab you from behind these buildings. It was real rough.

Then following that, we even took some UNRRA supplies for the Chinese, 500 miles up the Yangtze to as far as Hankow.*

Paul Stillwell: What kind of supplies were these?

Mr. Hair: Like food supplies. UNRRA was this relief organization by the government, you know, and it was mainly flour, big sacks of flour. We were loaded with that stuff. So we took that up to Hankow and around there.

Paul Stillwell: Did you beach quite a bit?

Mr. Hair: Yes, we beached in all those places—Amoy, Hong Kong, Shanghai, French Indochina, which is now Vietnam. Those places were rough.

Paul Stillwell: You probably got good at handling the ship.

Mr. Hair: Oh, yes. But the thing is, see, oftentimes Shanghai was off limits to us, because for many different reasons, I guess, they didn't like Americans. And as a result

---

* The United Nations Relief and Rehabilitation Administration (UNRRA) was established on 9 November 1943 by 44 nations to provide food, clothing, shelter, medical assistance, and other aid to the people of countries liberated from Axis control.

of that, when we could go ashore, many sailors were killed, and sometimes officers. They'd just reach out. You'd be walking down the street, around a building, and a guy would stab you in the back. It was a very bad relationship. This was when the Communists were trying to come in. A lot of different split groups there and all that. It was really bad. They hated Americans. So, as I said, at one time it was off limits to us. We couldn't go in there. The Whangpoo River in Shanghai was just like an open sewer. It was awful. In fact, if we tried to pour our garbage overboard, in these big cans, the sampans would get around there together to get some foodstuffs. It was really just that bad. It was really awful. You could see the country had just broken down under Chiang Kai-shek, and everybody was talking about how if something wasn't done, the Communists could come right in and take over, because they were advocating all this stuff like get rid of your rickshaws and all that. Why have an individual pull another individual? They were trying to win the people over to their side.

Paul Stillwell: And they succeeded.

Mr. Hair: Yea, they really did.* But we could see it coming. The Chinese soldiers were weak; they were just emaciated. But you talk about a beautiful sight. They had their women. Both the Communist troops and the Nationalist troops carried women with them. On those hot days, you could see them out there on the deck of that LST with all these beautiful umbrellas.

But each day we would have to throw one or two Chinese Nationalists overboard who had died of cholera. They didn't have much in the way of supplies; they just had rice. That was about it.

Paul Stillwell: So it was pretty crowded on board your ship?

---

* The Nationalist government of China, headed by Generalissimo Chiang Kai-shek, was in power until overcome by Communist forces led by Mao Tse-tung and backed by the Soviet bloc. The nationalists were then expelled to Formosa (later renamed Taiwan), and the Maoists established a new government on the mainland, the People's Republic of China, on 1 October 1949.

Mr. Hair: It was very crowded, very crowded. I was in charge of all the ammunition aboard ship during all those trips.

Paul Stillwell: Why were they on board your ship—for relocation?

Mr. Hair: Relocation.

Paul Stillwell: Were they refugees?

Mr. Hair: No, these were the soldiers.

Paul Stillwell: Oh, I see.

Mr. Hair: These were soldiers. But over there, the soldiers carried some of their women. They had women in the Army too. I guess they were more like nurses or something.

Paul Stillwell: Maybe they had some other duties too.

Mr. Hair: Yes, I'm sure they did. That's right.

Paul Stillwell: Did you get liberty in Hong Kong?

Mr. Hair: Oh, yes.

Paul Stillwell: That had been occupied throughout the war by the Japanese. What kind of shape was it in?

Mr. Hair: Oh, it was all bombed out. Ships were sunk in the harbor there. The only nice place there was over in Kowloon, the British side, across the harbor.

Paul Stillwell: The mainland.

Mr. Hair: Yes. We could go over there. They had some nice dancing over there, very nice dancing. I'll never forget, though, in Hong Kong, four or five of us went out together. You wouldn't dare go out by yourself. You went in a group of five or six. You had to be really careful. We got there, and they were selling these cats on the street, beautiful, silk ribbons on them of all different colors. But the thing was, what it was, they would sell them, and you'd take them to a hotel, and they would cook them for you. Because they didn't have much fresh meat or anything down there. So we were all drinking in there, and each one of us got ourselves a cat and went to the hotel to cook it. I was just drunk enough to eat it. It tasted good too. Yes. But we had many things up there.

Then we stopped over at Amoy, China. The British consulate was there. That was interesting. They've changed the name for that now.* I was reading in *The New York Times* that they had changed that town. It's no longer Amoy.

Paul Stillwell: Was there any special situation, either good or bad, as far as you being a black on that ship? How were you treated?

Mr. Hair: No. This was the second ship, now that I think about it, where I was the only black officer on that ship, the *LST-1026*. No, I had no trouble on there, no trouble at all, a wonderful skipper there. He was strictly military. He was one of these quiet guys who wouldn't talk to anybody. He was just the captain. You didn't talk to the captain. That sort of thing. But I had no problems there. We had one of our officers out there go berserk. He had no sense of humor, very serious, and one day he just went berserk all over the ship. Went to get his gun; he was going to kill everybody. We later tracked him and got him and sent him back to the States, fortunately for him. He wrote me some years later. He was in Sweden studying to be an engineer. So he had really recovered all right. But that's rough on a guy out there if he doesn't have some kind of tranquility to fall back on.

---

* A coastal city in southeastern China, the port formerly known as Amoy is now Xiamen.

Paul Stillwell: Were you giving any thought at that point to making a career of the Navy?

Mr. Hair: No, I really wasn't. I guess it goes back to the time I went into the Navy with the thought of enlisting for the duration, to serve my country as best I could during the war, but not to make it a career. So I just hadn't given it any other thought.

Paul Stillwell: By now, the war was over. Were you waiting for something so you could get out?

Mr. Hair: Yes. Of course, you had to have a certain number of points.*

Paul Stillwell: You hadn't reached that.

Mr. Hair: No, I hadn't reached that. I finally reached that and got out. You came the day after the anniversary of my discharge—November 11, 1946.

Paul Stillwell: So '46 was spent largely in that LST?

Mr. Hair: Yes, yes, right. It was. That was my last ship. On that ship, we took it over to Subic Bay, Manila. That's where we decommissioned that ship.

Paul Stillwell: Did you get involved in the decommissioning process there?

Mr. Hair: No. We just had to mainly take the ship there. They had someone else that took charge.

Paul Stillwell: How did you get back home then?

---

* For the demobilization of the U.S. armed forces after World War II, the services had a point system to determine individual priorities for leaving the service. Points were awarded for length of service, overseas service, battle stars, decorations, and dependent children. Those with the highest number of points were the earliest discharged.

Mr. Hair: Another troopship.

Paul Stillwell: I hope that was a better experience than going out.

Mr. Hair: It was. It was interesting.

Paul Stillwell: Did you have any definite plans when you became a civilian again and got back to the States?

Mr. Hair: Yes, I did. Of course, first of all, when I came back to the States, I was trying to get adjusted to civilian life again. One of the interesting things was, after I left San Francisco, came on back, I went to Fort Pierce, Florida. I thought two of my brothers and three sisters were living there at that time. I went there for a homecoming, and I was really elated, and I was really looking forward to seeing them with the greatest expectation. I was just imagining this happy time we were going to have at this reunion. I learned right after I got there that my brother had just been run out of town. I said, "Oh, what a homecoming." Oh, man. He was a mechanic, and he had disagreed with some white woman there about having fixed her car. It was one of those little trivial things, but anything like that could do it. They'd make all these threats of killing you, or, "You'd better get out of town by night." It was one of those things.

But anyway, so I went there, and I stayed there for a while, still trying to adjust. I said, "Well, I'll take a vacation first to sort of reorient myself to civilian life," which I did. But while I was around there then, I started looking around for jobs. It was very difficult in this little, small town. I couldn't locate anything. About the only thing that was available for a black person then was in the field of education, and I didn't have an education diploma. My main thing was social work, and, of course, nothing like that was open up to us yet at that time. Anyway, I stayed around there for quite a little while, and I really enjoyed it.

In the meantime, I was keeping up my contact with my future wife; she was my girlfriend at that time. Then through this contact, then she came down to see me a few times. At that time, after she finished, she had gotten a job, so she was living there in

New York. Since I couldn't find anything down there, then I said, "Oh, heck." Because I had always planned that I would probably end up in New York because the job opportunities were better than in Fort Pierce, which they were at the time. Certainly many more of them.

So, anyway, I came on to New York. At that time, I didn't get anything right away. I stayed on vacation for a while, getting used to things again. But eventually I found something through a friend of mine, where one of the stores was looking for somebody to work in the protection department. I think it was Bloomingdale's. I got on down there, and I started working in this for a while, but there was still the goal of getting into social work. But you really needed your master's in order to get into social work. You could get in on a lower level, but it didn't really pay. Plus your chances of advancement were very slim. So, anyway, I worked for a while.

In 1947, my wife and I got married. Oh, we had a heck of a family—a wonderful family—three children. Fortunately, we were able to put all of them through college. They did well. In fact, my oldest daughter was on the honor roll of [unclear] high School, which was a very competitive high school at that time, a straight-A student. So she went on to Syracuse and got into the foreign exchange program, studying languages, and studied at the University of the Andes in Bogota, Colombia, for a semester. Another one went on to Rochester. My son is now at Southern Illinois University. They all finished, and they're all doing well today.

Paul Stillwell: What sorts of work are they in?

Mr. Hair: My daughters right now have children, so they are just housewives. My oldest daughter has three now, twins and a little girl, so she is really kept busy there with them. They're doing all right. They live up in Stamford, Connecticut. Her husband is with First Boston, so they can afford to do that. My son is an insurance underwriter, and my other daughter is a housewife. So they're all doing fine.

But then in 1948, I matriculated at Fordham University School of Social Services and got my master's degree in social work, came out in 1950, and then I went right on into the field of social work. Subsequent to that, I went on to further my education at

New York School of Social Work, which is outstanding; it's part of Columbia University now. And then, as I said, I've stayed in the profession since then, ending up as the director of a social service agency over in Brooklyn. So that's been my professional background. Of course, on the side, as you know, I do recruiting for the Navy. I stay very busy now. I'm trying to do a family history or an autobiography, whatever it's going to be.

Paul Stillwell: What were some of the types of cases that you dealt with during this long career in social work?

Mr. Hair: We've had all kinds. For example, at one time I was with—in fact, I took part of my training there also, was the Jewish Board Gardens, Hawthorne Cedar Knolls School, which is a residential treatment center for very disturbed children. Then in that field there, I worked through clinics. Then I became quite an expert in the field of adoptions for this agency where I was. And then in the field of child welfare, counseling and things of that nature.

One of the interesting ones, though, was in the field of adoptions. I think it has brought about a lot of problems as a result of many of the policies that have developed in New York State pertaining to adoption, through their foster care program. So I've been in a lot of different aspects of social work.

Paul Stillwell: This surrogate motherhood is really a quandary.

Mr. Hair: Oh, yes. But adoption is a beautiful thing once you do it right. I was always a proponent of involving the biological parents and the adoptive parents in the adoption process. Once you do it that way and do it right, usually you have no problems. I know cases that we work through today, whereby the biological parents live in North Carolina, the adoptive parents live here, but each year they send that child down to see their biological mother, who has subsequently married somebody else. But it's that sort of thing, and it really helps the child with their own identity aside from many other things. But it's a terrific thing. I've never had one to backfire yet.

Paul Stillwell: That's a relatively recent development, isn't it? We've had all these sealed records.

Mr. Hair: That's right. But I was doing it even back then. But you had to do it on the QT. You couldn't do it in terms of agency policy, but you find people in your study, where they have no anxieties at all about the natural parents, so there you had a good subject, and you approach them on this, "What do you think of it?"

"Oh, yes, we would love it." This is the only way to do it. For the sake of the child. Because you can't love the child and hate the mother, or the parents, or the father. It's impossible. So we use this a lot with them.

But you get those who say, "No, don't you ever bring them. They're no good." You've really got a case. You could have problems if you're not careful. You could really have problems, because the one who is going to sense this first is going to be that child. "Look, you don't love my parents, so therefore you don't love me." You can't. That's tough to deal with. That's very tough.

Paul Stillwell: You're dealing with human lives and emotions.

Mr. Hair: But many parents would go along with that right away. They didn't mind that at all. But it was a very interesting field—still is. New York is unique in terms of its problems when it comes to child welfare. They've still got a lot of problems.

Paul Stillwell: And the black community has changed a great deal. Black and white, obviously. I was just reading an article in *The New York Times* recently that when the black communities were essentially self-contained, you had the upwardly mobile middle class lived right there and provided stability and leadership, and when they left, there was a real void.

Mr. Hair: Yes, that's true. Sometimes I wonder today what's going to happen to our middle class the way things are going now. They don't have enough places for these middle-income people to stay, a place where they can afford it. The same is true out in

Connecticut. *The Times* just did a study on Long Island here, Nassau and Suffolk counties, and because of that factor, young couples who are not having children are moving away, and the school population right here in Hempstead has dropped by 30% because of that factor. They can't afford the housing. They can't buy a house. It's really quite a problem.

Paul Stillwell: You did some work with the Seamen's Institute also, didn't you?

Mr. Hair: That was with the Society for Seamen's Children. It wasn't the Seamen's Institute. That's a different thing. The Seamen's Institute is a terrific place. But that was the agency I was director of. We had child welfare programs, family counseling, adoptions, and so forth.

Paul Stillwell: What are your overall views on the day-care business and how that relates to raising happy children and so forth?

Mr. Hair: If a person must go to work, the mother or father or whatever in this day and age—if the mother can't stay home with that child, and it's just one of those things that they can't do it, they have no other choice. I don't think it's a very good idea. That's why I'm so proud of my daughters today, where they stay home to raise their children. Not only that, but so many mothers who are going out to work, they're only making enough to pay for the care of the child in so many instances, so they're not gaining anything by it.

Paul Stillwell: What they're gaining is their personal satisfaction.

Mr. Hair: That's right.

Paul Stillwell: Their career. Maybe at the expense of their child.

Mr. Hair: Yes. It's a fact. I think this really could have its effect on that child. That's why another thing in the city of New York, in the agency where I was, I would take no child into care unless at least one parent—there had to be one parent, preferably two parents—who would participate in the entire process. I didn't feel that I was God, that I could go out there and play parent to this child. We had to have the parents there. I didn't give a damn whether they were on dope or alcohol or you name it. But the interesting thing about it, in my 30-something years there, I have never found to this day—one of these things that you see turn around so often, and I've never run across it—where I've found a parent, a biological, natural parent, who was not interested in their child, and I've seen them on dope, alcohol, no matter what.

But if you had the expertise to talk to them, to find out their feelings about this thing, I never found one yet who was not interested in their child. True, they could not laugh with that child, and that's without [unclear], but "We can help you with this stuff. We can do something about helping you get back on your feet." But I never found a parent who was not interested in their child. We see this so often, the publicity in the papers, "They're not interested, they don't care, they've done this, they abuse their child," and so forth. "The whereabouts of the parents are unknown," and all that, and, "We haven't seen them in years." But one of the interesting things about it is 95% of the children who come into foster care in the city of New York, like 25,000 or something like that, 95% came in on a voluntary placement plan, meaning that the mother or the father agreed to let that child come and signed papers. So you have to have the parents. If you say the whereabouts of the parents are unknown, they're unknown because you haven't been out there to see where they are, or made no attempt to.

Paul Stillwell: There's a potential for enormous satisfaction there to get a child started on the right path.

Mr. Hair: Oh, yes, no doubt about it. I remember one big black kid, about 6 feet, 6 inches tall—a big fellow. The first time I met him was in jail. I don't remember all the occasions, but we did a lot there. Maybe two or three years before I retired, I was walking down the street one day, and I felt someone behind me. He kept yelling, "Sir,

sir, sir." My first reaction was, "I'm going to get robbed here or something." Then I saw this big figure coming behind me. Then I turned around to look, and there was this fellow. He said, "Pardon me, but are you Mr. Hair?"

I said, "Oh, my goodness." I gave myself a sigh of relief, because I didn't know what was going to happen. I said, "Yeah."

He said, "Well, I am such and such a person. I owe you so much, and I owe you $5.00."

He had borrowed $5.00 from me. I couldn't imagine what this kid was talking about. I didn't know who he was. But, anyway, to make a long story short, he told me how I had met him in jail and how much I'd worked with him and his family and helped him out. You can't treat a child in a vacuum, so I'd always go to see the parents. And anyway, the situation straightened out. After that, I left. After about a year or two there in service, with them treating him, and I didn't see him anymore. He was still in high school, but he told me he was going to finish high school. Anyway, when I met him, he said he had just finished the University of Minnesota, and he was working in the planning division of the City of New York. You never know how many of those things would happen, but it really makes a difference.

Paul Stillwell: Of course, it does. What is your feeling on the overall subject of affirmative action? Do you think that's a good thing?

Mr. Hair: I think it is. I think affirmative action is very good, because, see, blacks have been denied things for so long. I think that in some of the situations, because there is still so much racism—for example, take our police department here in New York City. It's changing now, but going back a few years, only a handful of blacks could get in, and there were all kinds of ways of keeping you out, through tests or whatever you might say. In those situations, I think it's very good. I think from a constitutional point of view, where we say equal justice and equal rights under the law for all; we should all have equal opportunity and things like that. I think that would be good, but sometimes it just doesn't work in practice. Yet I recognize that sometimes it might have just an adverse effect, too, where we get discrimination in reverse. You have to be very careful about this. I think you have to take it not in terms of a broad kind of thing, but I think you have to take it individual by individual case and situation and use it for affirmative action.

Paul Stillwell: It's really seen as a remedy for past injustice.

Mr. Hair: In some situations, when you could find that there may not be any need for it, but I'm talking about those situations where there's really a need. I think something should be done. Like the case where the white fellow is suing because affirmative action kept him out of college or something like that, out of medical school.* You get all kinds of cases. But I think it does help to right some of the situations that have been long overdue.

Paul Stillwell: You've had a lifetime and been in many cases involved in serving others. Where does the Navy experience fit in that whole pattern and context?

Mr. Hair: In terms of serving others? I think the Navy has made a lot of strides, not that there isn't a lot of room still for improvement. There still is. But I think that in terms of what has happened over the years with the Navy, there's been a lot of improvement in it. There are areas now where we are still behind. For example, we're not getting enough black kids from high school on up. They're not going into the Navy. This is an area where we're sort of behind right now, as opposed to, say, the Marine Corps, and some of the others. But I think they've done a lot—what Harry Truman did and Lyndon Baines Johnson and the rest of them did in terms of integrating the services.† All of the services—the Navy and all of them. It's really a terrific thing. As one guy put it, it's just really a phenomenon in terms of integration. But under that controlled group, you can do it much better than you could in an open society in terms of integrating the services. The

---
* In the early 1970s Allan Bakke, a white male, sought admission to the medical school of the University of California Davis. He was denied entry while "special applicants" with lower scores were admitted through affirmative action. Bakke sued, and the case eventually went to the Supreme Court, which ruled in 1978 in his favor. It ruled that race could be a consideration in admissions but ruled against the setting of quotas.
† On 26 July 1948, President Harry S. Truman issued Executive Order 9981, which said, "It is hereby declared that there shall be equality of treatment and opportunity for all persons in the armed services without regard to race, color, religion, or national origin." In the mid-1960s President Lyndon Johnson fostered important civil rights legislation.

Navy is much more integrated than the society, and this was a problem all throughout the war, where the base was integrated, but the town wasn't. It really created a lot of problems. That's when Truman came along, and I think he was one of the most decisive Presidents we ever had. Of course, Lyndon Baines Johnson wasn't slow on it either. He was really terrific as opposed to the liberal type guy who gave you a lot of beautiful words but who wouldn't take any action. But these guys took action, and the record is right there.

Paul Stillwell: You had a long void, out of touch with the other fellows who were in the Golden Thirteen. Can you describe the getting back together with them?

Mr. Hair: Oh, that was fantastic. Oh, yes, a lot of wonderful things happened then. It was almost like a nightmare with me, one of those things I could just hardly believe. I'm sitting here on a Wednesday, I remember it so well, and I try to read a lot of papers, but I try to read the *Times* every day. One day I was reading the *Times*, and here was this picture of all these buddies of mine, the Golden Thirteen, out to sea on a cruise, had been there since Monday. The headline was something to the effect that "38th Reunion for First Black Officers Aboard the USS *Kidd*." It went on to describe this and what a wonderful reunion it was.* They said that there were only eight surviving members, and these were the ones that were in this reunion. So I pinched myself. I said, "I'll be damned. Look at here. Son of a gun." I said, "These guys out there, and they say only eight of us alive! I know I'm still alive." I pinched myself and said, "I know damn well I'm alive."

And so right away, my reaction was, "Let me go call this *New York Times*." I think a guy named Franklin was the writer on this story, so I went and called the *Times*. "Let me speak to Mr. Franklin."

They told me, "Oh, no, he's not here. He is in the Washington bureau of *The New York Times* in Washington, D.C."

---

* From 13 to 15 April 1982, the surviving members of the Golden Thirteen held a reunion on board the guided missile destroyer *Kidd* (DDG-993) at sea in the Atlantic. See PH2 Drake White, "Golden 13 Together Again," *All Hands*, August 1982, pages 8-11.

I said, "Oh, no." So they gave me his number anyway to call him down there. But, anyway, I thought about it. I said, "I don't want to call Washington, D.C. I know what I'm going to call—the Navy. But I'm not going to call just the Navy; I'm going to call Navy intelligence." So I got that number, and I called Navy intelligence. I told them that I had read the article in *The New York Times* about the Golden Thirteen and their reunion at sea aboard the USS *Kidd*, and I said, "I'm not with them, but I'm a member of the Golden Thirteen."

They said, "Huh?"

I said, "Yeah, I'm a member of the Golden Thirteen."

So they questioned me a little bit, maybe saying to themselves, "Is this guy from Bellevue or someplace?"[*]

So anyway, I kept insisting. I said, "No, I'm a member of that. I'm a member of the Golden Thirteen."

So they looked at the *Times* and said, "You sure?"

I said, "Yeah." So, anyway, they took my name and address and all that, and said, "Well, wait a minute." I guess they did some checking on that to make sure I wasn't from Bellevue.

So then the next thing I know, I started getting these calls from the national Navy headquarters there in Arlington. I must have gotten 15 or 20 calls.

Paul Stillwell: In one day?

Mr. Hair: Yes, all that day, and it was a different person. One person called and said he was calling from the White House. I don't remember his name or anything, because one was right after the other. But each one wanted to know the same thing. Just like we are doing here today, I had to go through my past history, where I was born, when I entered the Navy, what ships I served on, and blah, blah, blah. Naturally, they had to use this to identify me, to make sure that I wasn't just some crackpot or something.

So anyway, after about 20 calls, some captain or somebody on the other end of the phone said, "By golly, you are James Hair, aren't you?"

---

[*] Bellevue Hospital Center, just outside of New York City, is known for its psychiatric facilities.

I said, "I certainly am."

So then the next thing he said, "Can you travel?"

I said, "Oh, yeah, yeah, I'm able to travel."

He said, "Could you get ready in three hours, because we'll have somebody there to pick you up?"

I said, "Yeah." So I went up and got ready. Sure enough, within three hours, a Navy car pulled up out there. They took me over to La Guardia, put me on that airplane, flew me down to Norfolk.* I got there that night, late at night, and put me up there in a motel someplace. The next morning, I was flown by helicopter out to meet my buddies on the USS *Kidd*. I guess it was like 100 miles or so out, something like that.

Paul Stillwell: This would have been Thursday, then.

Mr. Hair: Yes, right. And I went there, and by this time, they had just told the guys that I was coming. I guess they figured it would be too much for these guys' hearts to take it. But anyway, so they put me down aboard this ship, and when I got off, I saw my buddies over there in one place. I was sort of looking around for the captain. I said, "I need to request permission to come aboard here," but I didn't see any captain. But anyway, I went on over there where they were, left this helicopter, and by that time, they started mugging me. I'll tell you, that was really something. That was a great time, really a happy time. Banging me over the head. They took my helmet off, and we just had a grand time. It was really something. It was just a lot of backslapping and hitting and hugging and all that stuff that went on there with those guys. It was really some enjoyment. You know, you just couldn't believe it!

Paul Stillwell: I wonder how come they had found everybody else but not you?

Mr. Hair: Some way or another, they said the Navy had misplaced my address, so I guess that was about it. They really misplaced my address.

---

* LaGuardia Airport is on Flushing Bay in the New York borough of Queens.

Paul Stillwell: And you've been with them every year since then.

Mr. Hair: Yes, that's right. I still say today they still owe me all those trips that they have taken. They went to San Diego, Orlando, Florida, New Orleans, and I think there was some other place—San Francisco, too, they had gone earlier. Four trips the Navy owes me on this. But that was really something.

Of course, after that, they took us on into the room there aboard that. Oh, that's some ship, that USS *Kidd*. Oh, we just had a grand time there, and where I'd been. White had prepared some legal document there for my burial at sea, because they thought I was dead and all that sort of stuff. The other guys thought I was passing. They didn't know where I was. But anyway, this went on and on. It was so funny, because then I asked Dalton Baugh, "Dalton, gee, I was looking for the captain to request permission to come aboard when I got here. Where was he?"

He said, "Man, he got sick when he saw you coming down here."

I said, "What happened?"

He said, "Well, you know, the USS Kidd was originally built for the Shah of Iran."* It's a luxurious ship. He said, "When he saw you coming down there, he thought for sure you were the reincarnated Shah of Iran coming back to take over his ship." Oh, we had some fun out there, though.

Paul Stillwell: It sounds like it.

Mr. Hair: But that was some great reunion. I never will forget that.

Paul Stillwell: I take it that you still keep your hand in by doing some recruiting for the Navy.

---

* Four ships that were guided missile variants of the *Spruance* (DD-963) class were ordered for delivery to Iran when the Shah was in power. After Iran's government fell to the Ayatollah Ruhollah Khomeini in 1979, the ships were completed for the U.S. Navy. The USS *Kidd* (DDG-993) and her three sisters went into commission in 1981 and 1982.

Mr. Hair: Oh, yes. In fact, this guy just called a little while ago to speak at a junior high school. It was all about the Navy, blacks in the Navy, how things have changed, the different opportunities today—all that sort of stuff. We don't do any follow-through in terms of who goes in, but we know we're getting quite a number through the process. And that's the way the Navy's using us now, on that sort of national level.

Paul Stillwell: With the benefit of hindsight, could you reflect on the historic role that you and the others have had in the Navy?

Mr. Hair: In the Navy.

Paul Stillwell: At the time, you said you were too busy to reflect, but you've had that time now.

Mr. Hair: It's true that we were the guys, the fellows who paved the way, so to speak, in the Navy. There's certainly no doubt that we did a lot of things there. We had to do a lot of things in order to get where we got, and I'm sure that we accomplished a lot by it. But the way I look at it is that with all of our achievements, which were great, I think, in view of the situation at that time, because Mr. Jim Crow ran the Navy in that time. The Navy was a Jim Crow outfit. But with all of this that took place and all that we did, I really don't look at it from a personal point of view.

I look at it more in terms of the fact that I did this because there were 160,000 other guys out there in the Navy, and we did it because not only that, but you had many people out there, like Dr. Mary McLeod Bethune, the NAACP, and you had many white people along with the different groups, who were fighting to do everything possible to get open enlistment for all people of the United States, in accordance with our constitutional rights and that sort of thing. So when it comes to this sort of thing, I feel that I really should thank all those people back there that I knew, and most of all my parents, who started me out on the right way. Then I had all these other people there as extensions of my parents who followed through with the ideals about education, and accomplishments of civil rights and so forth. And in that respect, I think that it really has meant a lot.

I think it has meant a lot to this country in breaking down a lot of these things, the racist ideas that have existed for so long in the service of our Navy, in a Navy that goes back to a time when they've always had blacks, you know. Right from the beginning, there have always been blacks. A distant relative of mine, Robert Smalls, from South Carolina, during the Civil War days, took that ship and turned it over to the federal forces—the *Planter*. He was a distant relative. As I told you, my mother's maiden name was Rosa Nix. She was from South Carolina.

But in perspective, I think we were chosen to lead the way. With the support and help that we've gotten all along the way, we were able to do it, but we couldn't have done it without that support.

Paul Stillwell: Judge White said he felt that the Navy could have many, many times picked out groups of dozens of capable individuals, but the fact is that they picked out you. You had the opportunity, and you made the most of it.

Mr. Hair: I agree with Sylvester, too, that truly there were many other blacks out there that they could have gotten at that time, but they chose us. As fate would have it, we were the ones that were chosen, and we did the job.

Paul Stillwell: One of the most important things you can do is to be an individual and to show people what that individual can do, as opposed to a stereotype.

Mr. Hair: Yes, right. Absolutely. Absolutely. This we did. This is why I say that, as I've heard people talk about heroes and what it means to be a hero. Maybe a year ago, I was reading about this guy in the Navy, I can't remember his name now, who broke the Japanese code. I think they just honored him.[*]

Paul Stillwell: Joe Rochefort.

---

[*] In the early part of World War II, Commander Joseph J. Rochefort, USN, successfully led a team of cryptanalysts based at Pearl Harbor, Hawaii. Their work had a key role in U.S. Navy successes against the Japanese. Rochefort later retired from active naval service as a captain and died in 1976. In 1985 he was posthumously awarded the Navy Distinguished Service Medal.

Mr. Hair: That's right. Joe Rochefort. I think he's deceased now.

Paul Stillwell: Yes, he is, but he did not get the honor in his lifetime.

Mr. Hair: Now there's a guy who was a hero.

Paul Stillwell: Yes.

Mr. Hair: That's a guy who was a hero, so you have to sort of redefine what you mean by a hero. A hero doesn't have to be somebody who goes out there and sinks a ship, but a hero is in terms of our country, in many, many ways. That's why I say that with me, and I think the other guys, it was the same thing, our goal became our precedent over any sort of Jim Crowism or whatever it is.

Paul Stillwell: It's been a real pleasure and a privilege for me to talk to you and the other members of that group who are still alive. I salute your accomplishment, and I'm grateful for your making this contribution.

Mr. Hair: Thanks a lot. It's the same here with you. I really appreciate it. There's another thing. I can't quote it exactly, but Paul Laurence Dunbar wrote a poem. To sort of paraphrase it, he said that, "O Lord, we pray not . . ."[*]

---

[*] The interview tape ended in mid-sentence. African American Paul Laurence Dunbar (1872-1906) wrote a celebrated poem titled "The Warrior's Prayer." One stanza reads:

"I do not ask that thou shalt front the fray,
And drive the warring foeman from my sight;
I only ask, O Lord, by night, by day,
Strength for the fight."

Interview Number 2 with Mr. James E. Hair, Member of the Golden Thirteen
Place: Mr. Hair's home in Hollis, New York
Date: Thursday, 10 November 1988

Paul Stillwell: Here we are again, Mr. Hair. It's almost exactly two years to the day since our first meeting. Then it was the day after Veterans Day, and now in 1988 it's the day before. At that time you discussed your colleagues in the Golden Thirteen, and we now want to go into a little more detail on each one, please.

Mr. Hair: Yes, I would, and I especially want to thank you again for coming back. It's just wonderful having you here. And, certainly, again I'm very glad to participate.

First, I'd just like to add a little bit more on some of the persons who were members of the Golden Thirteen and who were with me in the class, Officer Candidate School out at Camp Robert Smalls, Great Lakes, Illinois.

I'll start off with Jesse Arbor. Jesse in the group was, to me, a most self-confident person. He used to portray to us that we didn't have a thing to worry about, just go ahead and do what you have to do, and everything would be okay. He was the type of guy in the group who was always ready to share, and he was never lacking in something to talk about. He was always ready and willing to contribute to the group.

Again, with Judge White, William Sylvester White, he came to the group with a background in politics. His father had been active in Chicago politics, and this certainly added a new dimension to our group there. He brought an awareness of the importance of the news media, particularly as it related to the Negro at that time. He was quite a positive force in the group with us there at Camp Robert Smalls.

Paul Stillwell: How did that positive force manifest itself?

Mr. Hair: In terms of helping us to be aware of just what we were doing at that time and what it would mean in terms of the media, and how we should be thinking about this in terms of our own conduct and our own behavior because of the situation at that time.

The other person I'd just like to mention a little bit more about was Goodwin. I believe I mentioned this a little before, but Goodwin seemed to fit the need to keep Commander Armstrong abreast of what was happening in and around our group and the Officer Candidate School. It was quite obvious that Commander Armstrong had a great need for this, and Goodwin carried out this service in a very effective manner. Also, it served to keep our nose to the grindstone, so to speak, because Goodwin never would let any of us get out of line. To illustrate that point, I think I mentioned before something about one time we attempted to shoot dice and Goodwin was not present at the time, but later came and immediately stopped the game. It was that sort of thing, because Goodwin thought very strongly that this was not becoming of an officer to shoot dice.

Another very good friend in the group there was Dalton Baugh. Dalton was a most diligent and determined person to fill the assigned task that was given to him. Even after we had solved the problem, he would pursue it further and with pertinent questions. He seemed to have had a background in research. He was very patient in his search for the knowledge and constantly pursued this in a most meticulous and learned fashion. He was indeed a wonderful person who contributed greatly to our group.

Dennis Nelson was an individualist. He was a feisty, independent person, who was able to stay under control during all of our training there. He shared in the group discussions and made many wonderful contributions. It was interesting how after we became officers, he changed and went out to demonstrate his independent and feisty ways.

Paul Stillwell: Well, it must have taken a lot of self-discipline then to keep himself under control.

Mr. Hair: It certainly did at that time. It really did. Of course, we were limited in a way there, because we couldn't go out. We had no liberty or anything of that nature, so I think that served to really keep Nelson under control very well.

Paul Stillwell: Well, but he could have, for example, shown off in the group itself.

Mr. Hair: Yes, yes. He could have. He could have. But he more or less kept himself under control. I can't think of anything right now where I could say that he really showed off in the group. But he was quite different. There was no doubt about it; he was quite different.

Paul Stillwell: Well, every member of the group that I've talked to had his own favorite Dennis Nelson story. What are yours?

Mr. Hair: I can't remember any particular story. The only thing that sticks out right now about Dennis Nelson was he was really concerned about getting his transcript from college because, without that transcript from college, he wasn't going to be able to stay in the group. And, of course, this was made known to him in no uncertain ways. But what was holding up his transcript was an outstanding debt that he still owed his college. Of course, he recognized that he had to pay that debt in order to stay in the group. And I understand he did, and then they released his transcript. But that was the main thing that I remember about him at the time. And, of course, aside from what the other fellows have said about him. But he was a unique individual, no doubt about it.

The next person I have here is John Reagan. John to me was a somewhat quiet person in the group, but he did contribute to it. He was a good listener and would participate in the group on different matters that we would discuss pertaining to the class subjects. As you know, later on John came to join me on board the tug after we were commissioned. It was a few months after I was aboard there John came over, and he served as the exec on board the tug.

Well, during that time we did a lot of different things with the tug. I never will forget one day we got orders to go to the Brooklyn Navy Yard and take a scow out in the ocean for dumping. We did, and I guess we must have had out about 400 feet of line hooked onto that scow. We took it out to the ocean and after dumping it we started back. At this time I was exhausted, so I asked John to relieve me, which he did. So I went down below to sleep. I guess I hadn't slept about 48 hours or so. And I went down below to take a nap. The next thing I knew, John called me and told me that they were lost. When I came up to the pilothouse, I looked out, and there was this heavy fog there. It was like milk. You couldn't see more than about five feet or so in front of you. It was very heavy, very thick fog. And no one could tell me where they had seen the last marker or fix or anything of that nature. My first reaction was that I wanted to get angry, but I said to myself, "Oh, heck, no. That's not going to help the situation." I said, "Gee, we've got to get out of here and . . ."

I knew we weren't too far from Long Island, and something else—we could end up on the rocks. So what I did right away was run outside, outside the pilothouse. I got down as close to the water as I could and I looked at the water to see what the color was, also to see how the waves were breaking. And, of course, in the meantime I was feeling the wind to see how powerful it was and where it was setting us down, and the currents and all of that. Immediately, when I saw the color of the water and the waves breaking short, I yelled up before I could get back to the pilothouse, "Turn hard left." We went on that course for a while and then I kept watching the wind and the water until eventually the fog cleared. And when it cleared, by the help of the good Lord, we were right at the entrance of Ambrose Channel coming into New York Harbor. It was one of the luckiest moves I ever had in my life, because all the guys thinking we were going to end up on those rocks over there some place. But that was it. And there was this huge scow still behind us. So that was one of the luckiest breaks we ever had.

Paul Stillwell: It sure gives your crew a lot of confidence in you when you do something like that.

Mr. Hair: I would hope so. But John was there; John always remembers that incident that we had there. He never could figure out how he got wrong on that day.

Paul Stillwell: Did you have radar on that tug?

Mr. Hair: Oh, no. No radar, no radar then at all.

One of the other persons that always gave me a deep sense of pride to talk about is Graham Martin. And I should say along with this is Alma, his wife. Because Graham, in the group, was just a first-class student and a dynamic individual. He was an exceptional person, and he did not speak quickly in the group. He thought about what he was going to say. He thought it through first, and he contributed very well on all the subject matters that we had. And it was most interesting because, as I said, he didn't talk often, but whenever Graham spoke, everybody got quiet and would listen. Because what he had to contribute to that group was most meaningful and was most helpful on the particular subject matters that we were discussing at that time. He is a wonderful guy and the same goes for Alma, his wife.

Paul Stillwell: You told me that he was a special friend of yours in the group. How did that come about?

Mr. Hair: I wish I could really put it in words. I really don't know. I guess it just came about, not at any one moment but over the years. And seeing Graham and being around with such a genuine person, I got to feel his sincerity. Not only his, but also with Alma. And how sincere and dedicated persons they were. It was as though if one said something, it was just the same as if the other one said it. So, and like it is today, when I called them or when Graham was in the hospital I called him, and I would alternate the calls. Once I called Alma and once I called Graham. As I told them, "If I talk to either one of you, I know I was talking to both of you." It's just that sort of thing. And it's that way with them. They are just great people there together—two wonderful people together. I admire them, but I think it just came about over the years and knowing him, and somehow or other, one day it just clicked. He and I just became very close together.

Paul Stillwell: Did you have that feeling when you were undergoing the training together, or did it come later?

Mr. Hair: No, it came later. It really came later. I knew some of it was there when we were undergoing training, but I didn't have the awareness of it until later on. In fact, he's written me some beautiful letters, beautiful letters. He keeps me up to date on his situation, but never in a complaining fashion, he or Alma.* Neither one of them complain. And the other week I talked with him. And they're really excited and they're looking forward to our next conference in Long Beach, California. They feel very positive about it and so do I.

Paul Stillwell: I hope they can make it.

Mr. Hair: Yes, right. So do I. I do. I think they will; I think they will. They couldn't make it to our last conference in Atlanta, Georgia, but we had the opportunity there to hook up a company phone, and we all talked to them from Atlanta, Georgia, at their home in Indianapolis. So they're really a wonderful group of people. Yes, indeed.

Another person I'd just like to add a little bit more about is Charles Lear, who was the warrant officer in the group. Whenever I think of Charles Lear, the thing that comes to mind right away is a statue of a military soldier. Lear was that image. He was really a real military man, in every sense of the word. Just to look at him he looked like a tough, bronze-type guy. He was ready to go out there and take on any kind of thing, and he lived this every day. Before coming into the group, I think he was into training out at boot camp to really get the guys into good shape for military battles, that type guy. I don't think they could have picked a better guy for that type of job than Charles Lear.

Charles and I also became very close friends over the years, and I got to know his wife also. He was just a wonderful guy, and he was always ready to adhere to and to follow all military procedure. He was a real asset to the Navy.

Paul Stillwell: I've sort of gathered from what people in the group have said, that if you made a list of people who loved the Navy, that Lear would be at the top of that list.

Mr. Hair: Yes, yes. That's right.

---

* In his later years Graham Martin had problems with his knees because of old football injuries, and Alma Martin was essentially immobilized because of multiple sclerosis.

Mr. James E. Hair, Interview #2 (11/10/88) – Page 122

Paul Stillwell: Apparently, it was the fact that the Navy wouldn't take him for a career that they really did him in.[*]

Mr. Hair: Yes. I think that's it. I think that really, that broke his heart in a way, you know, because this was his Navy. This was his Navy, and he was 100% Navy all the way. He was just that type of guy, a wonderful guy, and he made his contribution.

Paul Stillwell: How would you describe his contribution?

Mr. Hair: You're referring to just in the group there or throughout?

Paul Stillwell: Well, both really.

Mr. Hair: Actually, because throughout he was this military man that when orders came down to do something, Lear was there to do it. He was going to carry it out. He didn't ask any questions. He just knew that this had to be done because it was orders. He knew that orders were right, and this was what we had to do. He gave that sort of leadership in the group. And certainly a lot of this wore off onto others in the group there with us.

Paul Stillwell: Sort of leadership by example.

Mr. Hair: That's right.

Paul Stillwell: When you think about Lear and Arbor going out to the Pacific together, that's almost the odd couple.

Mr. Hair: Yes, that's right.

Paul Stillwell: Because Arbor's sort of the other way. He'd figure out his own way to get something done.

---

[*] Lear died shortly after the war, apparently by suicide.

Mr. Hair: Yes. Yes, right. But not Lear. Lear was a terrific guy, like I've heard the expression, something to the effect that not all heroes are made on the battlefield, the thunder and lightning of a military battle. Well, Lear could be that type of guy in many different situations, whether it's training people to go out to do battle, or just sitting in a classroom personifying what a good military man should be like. He was that type of person.

Paul Stillwell: What was his contribution during the training period?

Mr. Hair: He shared in many of the discussions there. I think if anything, you mean to say that he would hold back, but I think that one of the things was he was a learner in the group more than a contributor. And I guess this is understandable. I think Lear's one of the guys who never had any college training or anything of that nature. I don't think he did. So he was there to learn. And I'm sure he did learn.

Paul Stillwell: Well, that would, understandably, be sort of intimidating when you've got master's degrees and bachelor's degrees and so forth among the other officer candidates.

Mr. Hair: Right. Right. Right. Not that he didn't have a lot to contribute. He did. But as I say, he was more of a learner in that group, and a guy who provided a lot of leadership.

Paul Stillwell: How did that leadership demonstrate itself? In things that were in his experience, for example?

Mr. Hair: Yes.

Paul Stillwell: How would he do that?

Mr. Hair: Well, for example, every day we were on schedule. Say, for example, we were supposed to be up at, say, 0500, or whatever it is, Lear was going to be the first one on the deck. He was that type of person. And if we had to, say, turn in at a certain hour, Lear was going to be the first one there to do it. He was that sort of thing. If we had to study for so long, he was there to do that. He was one of the first in.

Paul Stillwell: My guess is that his uniform was always impeccable too.

Mr. Hair: Oh, no doubt about it. He was a neat guy. No doubt about it, yes. He was a wonderful person.

So I think that's mainly the highlights there on Charles Lear.

The other fellow I'd like to mention about something briefly is Sam Barnes. Sam was a guy who willingly shared in the discussions there. He really contributed quite a bit in the different subjects that we would talk about. He was a person who really wanted to make sure that we all stuck together, and that we all learned together, and that we would all grill one another about different subjects and so forth. He followed right along and pursued this in our group discussions there as we went along. So in that sense he made quite a wonderful contribution there to us.

Now that was Sam Barnes. Of course we had another one, Phillip Barnes. Phillip was the person who seemed always anxious to share in the discussions and things of that nature. Whatever he could bring to the group, he was always willing to do it. And very cooperative in every sense of the word. I considered him just another wonderful member of the group there.

Paul Stillwell: Would you call him anxious in the sense of insecure?

Mr. Hair: As I look back on it, I don't know whether it was insecurity or just what it was at that time. Because it's very difficult to remember things, going back 40-some years ago. I don't know if it was acting insecurely or what. I know that he was concerned about his weight, because he had a weight problem. Maybe there was some insecurity in there in that sense. I don't know. As I said, though, he would make his contributions. But it's difficult to remember everything about him. I know he was concerned about his weight. And, of course, being in the military in those days you couldn't go around overweight. That was a sign that you were not really in condition and so forth. That just wasn't tolerated. That's about all I can remember right now about Phillip Barnes.

Paul Stillwell: The three people that I think of that wouldn't strike me as insecure would be Cooper, White, and Sam Barnes. I'm wondering how he might compare with them, for example.

Mr. Hair: Cooper, White, Sam Barnes?

Paul Stillwell: How would Phil Barnes compare with that group?

Mr. Hair: Now, I wouldn't put him in the group with White, and Sam Barnes, and Cooper, and the rest of the fellows, no.

Paul Stillwell: They were all very self-confident and assured and . . .

Mr. Hair: Yes. Right. So, Phillip Barnes wouldn't fit into that group. So in that sense you might say he certainly was not as secure as they were. No.
And then after that, I mentioned Cooper. In the group I saw George as somewhat slow but deliberate person in the group discussions. He made his contributions to the group, and he always had a lot of questions, which was most helpful on different subject matters.

Paul Stillwell: Would it be fair to say that he had a more skeptical approach to things than some of the others?

Mr. Hair: I would think so. I would think so. I think that was rather the sense that came through with George and, I guess, this was probably reflected in a part of his history that he gave. I think he was skeptical and said he didn't know what was going to happen and so forth. Guess maybe he found this in the service later on in the capacities in which he served.

Paul Stillwell: It was sort of like "Can we really trust the Navy on this thing?"

Mr. Hair: Yes. Right. Right.

Paul Stillwell: What was your own feeling on that? Did you think the Navy could be trusted?

Mr. Hair: Oh, yes. In terms of the Officer Candidate School?

Paul Stillwell: Yes. Did you think they were making a good-faith effort to make officers of the group?

Mr. Hair: Oh, yes. I think they were. I didn't have any hesitation in terms of them following through with this program. Whether all of us would make it, I always felt that not all of us were going to make it in the group, because I was aware of Navy programs previous to this. They would start a program with 200 men, and before they started the program, they would say, "Well, we're going to have 50 wash out."

So I went in there with the awareness I that, if there were 16 of us, I didn't think 16 of us were going to graduate. I thought they were going to pick the top so many, but I didn't know who, how many that was or anything at that time. So in that sense, I felt very comforting about it when I went there, because I never had any idea that the Navy would go so far as to go through all of this study and all of this work and time-consuming efforts to get a group of blacks here for the Officer Candidate School—do all this background work and all that, and not come up with something. I just never felt that way about the Navy.

Now, just who were going to be the guys to complete the course or not, that was another thing. I didn't know. I thought that would depend on many different things there in that group. And, of course, the top thing was how we produced in that class.

Paul Stillwell: Since you didn't feel that everybody was going to make it, did you feel a sense of competition to try to make sure that you would be one of the ones who did?

Mr. Hair: Oh, yes, I did. I did. I felt that I was going to do the best I could, and I think everybody in the group there, more or less, felt that same way. That was my impression of them. Whoever did the best were the ones that were going to come out on top. A lot of other things that the Navy had done like with our background studies and things of that nature, I think they were going to take all that into consideration also.

Paul Stillwell: But you wouldn't do anything, though, I take it, to consciously put down another member so you could succeed.

Mr. Hair: Oh, no, no, no. Definitely not. No, no, I wouldn't do that. I wouldn't do that at all. No.

This is why I speak about the group as I did there. For example, just to list one. There were many of this way, but like Graham Martin—he is a guy of honesty, dignity, and integrity. You know what I mean? He wouldn't go there and knock down Jim Hair just to get him to suffer here, or something like that. You know what I mean? That's my feeling about Graham. I think this was true of many of the guys in that group.

Paul Stillwell: Well, he's the kind of a person you wouldn't feel comfortable knocking down.

Mr. Hair: No, no. That's true. That's true.

But it was a wonderful experience. Back to the main question, I don't see the Navy as bringing us all together here without something positive coming out of it. And this is the way it was. Particularly at that time, because, unless you've lived through those days, it is most imperative to try to get some understanding of what our country was like in those days. It is almost indescribable, like we hear a lot about apartheid and things of that nature, and see some of the ramifications of it. At least we learn a little bit about it. But in our country at that time, having black officers in the Navy was something almost foreign. It was a very difficult thing. It was quite an experiment that was put on by the Navy at that time. Of course, it was with the help of many people throughout the community and people from many walks of life that made this all possible.

Paul Stillwell: Well, there were certainly parts of this country that had what you could describe as apartheid at that time.

Mr. Hair: Yes. Right, right. And I think this was reflected in the letters that people wrote to *Life* magazine after they'd published the picture of us back there in 1944.* As I recall now, that *Life* magazine published this wonderful picture of these first 13 black officers in the Navy. They just listed them as the first Negro officers, but they didn't give any names in the caption.

Paul Stillwell: That's what struck me when I looked at it.

Mr. Hair: There were no names there at all. Just . . .

Paul Stillwell: These aren't individuals; it's just a category.

Mr. Hair: No, just 13 colored guys, 13 Negroes in those days. And that's the way it was. I think this, in a way, sort of relates to what I'm trying to bring out here in terms of the country at that time. And *Life* magazine was reflecting that in that picture, and also later in many of the letters to the editor of *Life* magazine. It was really giving testimony to what we were like in those days.

Paul Stillwell: You were being viewed in that picture in terms of color rather than as individuals.

Mr. Hair: Yes. That's right. That's right. And the first "coloreds," let's say, come into a Navy that up to then had in those days no colored officers. And I'm sure it was a very traumatic thing to a lot of people. Could be both ways.

---

* "First Negro Ensigns," *Life*, 24 April 1944, page 44. The 15 May 1944 issue of *Life* magazine published a series of letters in response to the photo of the black ensigns, and the issue also contained an editorial titled "Negro Rights." The pro and con responses in the letters represented some of the prevailing attitudes on race relations of the period.

Paul Stillwell: That's right.

Mr. Hair: Both ways for many different groups.

Paul Stillwell: Dr. Barnes put his tongue in his cheek and he said, "That's what killed Frank Knox."[*]

Mr. Hair: Yes, yes.

I never will forget a story that they told in my family about this. One of my older sisters at the time was coming home, and one of the neighbors called her. She had just gotten one of the papers. It was a local hometown paper, and it said up at the top there, "James Hair Navy Ensign." So this neighbor called her over, and she was crying profusely. She said, "Oh, no, lookie here what happened to your brother. Oh, what did the Navy do to him?"

She was crying profusely, so my sister kept after her, said, "Oh, Miss Jones, what's wrong, what's wrong?"

She said, "Look what the Navy did to James. They drove him insane."

Well, I'm just bringing this out to show how everybody was really upset about this. She wasn't acquainted with that word "Ensign" at that time.

But we have come a long way. Now I go around to the different schools here, because I serve in what they call a role model volunteer program. I go over every year during Black History Month and talk about the Navy, what it used to be and what you can do in the Navy now. And it's amazing sometimes the reaction that you get there.

Paul Stillwell: What sort of reactions do you get?

Mr. Hair: Well, the kids are really excited about it, but the interesting thing is they know nothing about the history of the Navy and the role of blacks in the Navy. They knew

---

[*] Frank Knox (1874-1944) ran unsuccessfully for Vice President of the United States in 1936. He was publisher of the *Chicago Daily News* when made Secretary of the Navy in 1940. He was recalcitrant about bringing black sailors and officers into the Navy. Knox died in office 28 April 1944, just over a month after the Golden 13 were commissioned.

nothing about it. Sometimes when you relate this to them, they seem to not believe you. But then what I usually do is take along a lot of pictures, and the pictures tell the stories. The pictures from the *Life* magazine and some of the letters that were written in *Life* magazine. They start seeing this, and then they start questioning, "Did that really happen?" That sort of thing. And eventually it gets to them, that they start coming around that this really happened.

But the other thing is now you can be here if you want to be in the Navy. And they start looking at it in a sort of historical fashion. It wasn't always this way, but now we can do these things, which is a great step. I think this is what we need more of now.

Paul Stillwell: Well, it is sort of human nature to take things for granted as they are.

Mr. Hair: Yes, yes. Yes, that's right. That's right.

I remember once there the Navy sent over other people to a school. One fellow there was a photographer, and a girl there was a news writer for the Navy, and things of that nature. Then the students started to identify with them, "Oh, you can write. Oh, you can do this in the Navy, and you can be a photographer in the Navy. You can do these sorts of things." And that had a lot of meaning to them.

Paul Stillwell: You can be a hero to these kids. Who were your heroes when you were growing up?

Mr. Hair: My hero when I was growing up? I guess I had many heroes when I was growing up. Of course, I always say that two of my greatest heroes, really, were my parents, because they started me out right.

My dad was a minister, and my mother was right there with him. And, of course, there were 21 brothers and sisters in the family. But that's what was, because they started us out right with the work ethic and "Do unto others as you would have them do unto you," "Love your neighbors as yourself." Not that they preached it so much, but they lived that life, and it was from living it that was really the greatest teacher I ever saw. So with that, I always say today that since then I've met a lot of great people and wonderful heroes and leaders in my lifetime, but it all stemmed from them. And these other great people I met since then through high school. I had some outstanding teachers at Lincoln Park Academy. William Paige, I'll always remember him. Outstanding guy that gave leadership and taught, too, at the same time. And, of course, after that was Dr. Mary McLeod Bethune, who was just an outstanding leader in that day and age.

I don't know of another leader at that time who would stand up for justice and the rights of all fellowmen as Mrs. Bethune did. I just never knew that. It was the only school that I went to in that day and age that did not tolerate racism and discrimination. That's right, she did not. With programs and all that, I went to other schools and they said that you can go this way, but you can only sit over here, and so forth. But not Mrs. Bethune. And this was the first school I went to back in the '30s.

At the same time we had set up an intercollegiate council there to have discussion groups between other colleges like Rawlings College in Florida, Stetson University, [unclear]—these were white colleges there—to discuss the social issues, the racial issues. But this was all because of Mrs. Bethune. It was a wonderful thing. One of the best cities I've ever lived in was Daytona Beach, Florida, because of Mrs. Bethune. It was terrific; the programs we had in the parks and all that were just great. The people there really got along—not that we didn't have a few incidents. We did, but they were very minor and very limited. But I'd never seen anything like that for that day and age. I'd have to go back to say it was really because of Mary McLeod Bethune.

Paul Stillwell: Do you remember any specific facets of her personality or her leadership traits?

Mr. Hair: Well, one of the first things she did, and which I see some of the other college presidents now doing--and one I might mention, because it was just in the news down at Spelman College with Dr. Johnnetta Cole.[*] With every student that comes to that school, I understand that she makes it her business to meet that student, to get to know that student. Well, I can say she got this from Mrs. Bethune. Now I don't know whether she

---

[*] Dr. Johnnetta Cole, an anthropologist, was the first black woman to serve as president of Spelman College in Atlanta. She held that post from 1987 to 1997.

did or not, I'm just thinking. I'll never forget that a few days after I got to Bethune-Cookman, Mrs. Bethune was busy with the Roosevelts and the Roosevelt administration there.[*] She spent a lot of time in Washington, D.C. But she was always back at the college frequently.

One day I was walking to one of the classes. She spotted me, and she looked over and said, "Hey, young man, young man. Come here." She said, "What is your name?" She wanted to know me, where I was from, what about my family. She wanted to know all these things. She'd take time out for these sorts of things. Then she looked at me, ready to give me a little tap on the shoulder and say, "Oh, you're going to do fine." That was Dr. Mary McLeod Bethune. Then after that, whenever time permitted, she would do the same thing. She would get around and talk to some of the student body there. She was a terrific person.

While we are on that subject, I'm just taking out a picture here I want to show you. I'm sure it would mean nothing to you just looking at it. But as you can see on the back here, it says "Christmas 1938. To my student friend James Hair. John G. Van Ness. December 6, 1852 to December 6, 1938." It was his birthday, and he was 86 years of age. But I mention this because Mrs. Bethune, as I mentioned, had many programs there at school. Every Sunday we had our services there. And the place was always packed. It had almost every ethnic group, but in that day we'd say we were black and white integrated in that auditorium. And many of these people became like supporters to us, like your big brother or something to help you. Well, John Van Ness and his wife took me on as one of their student friends to encourage me to continue. And I might say for the record, he's white.

Paul Stillwell: Was he a faculty member?

Mr. Hair: No, just a visitor and just a supporter of that school. We had black and white who would do these sort of things to encourage you on, and to do these sorts of things. So this picture here is one that I've always had and I've always cherished because he sent me this on his 86th birthday. His wife died shortly after, and today I don't know

---

[*] Eleanor Roosevelt (1884-1962) was the socially conscious wife of President Franklin D. Roosevelt.

whatever happened to that family. I don't know if they have children or what. I think that they do but where they are, I don't know. I've lost contact.

Paul Stillwell: Was he from Florida?

Mr. Hair: Yes, he was from Florida at that time.

Paul Stillwell: Well, from what you describe of Mrs. Bethune, it sounds as if she had a quality that President Roosevelt had also, to speak to an individual and make you feel like you were the only other person in the world.

Mr. Hair: Oh, there's no doubt about it. There's no doubt about it. She was just that way. And she would tell us many things about herself, and the things that she liked, and so forth. But always encouraging you on. Whenever she had time, she'd come out on campus. It was only on occasion. I wouldn't say she did that many times, because she was such a busy person.

I remember one day we were out there. We were all sitting around singing. She heard, and she came out to join in. It was a song that she liked so well, so she always asked us to sing it to her. It was "Let Me Call You Sweetheart."

Paul Stillwell: That goes back a ways.

Mr. Hair: Yes, yes, it does. She was some terrific person. On the sad side of it—I never will forget it—on occasion she told us about how she was getting older now and one day she would pass away. She said, "You see that oak tree right over there? That's where I want to be buried, right by that oak tree." She used to say many times, you know, "Shoot for the moon, shoot for the moon, keep going." She was a really, quite a motivator and a person that you would want to try to emulate. This is why I'm saying that I'm so thankful to my parents, and she was really an extension of my parents.

Paul Stillwell: Sounds like she was a hero or heroine to you.

Mr. Hair: Yes, she really was. She was really terrific.

Paul Stillwell: And an inspiration.

Mr. Hair: Yes. And I met many people that way, many people that way.

I've got a very dear friend of mine; in fact, I heard from him recently. I've got a folder there that I keep his letters in. His name is Charles Beckner; I call him Bill. Bill Beckner and I grew up in the same town. He was a grade or two behind me in school. I don't know why he said this, and I asked him and he passed it off every time I asked him about it. But I'd gone to Bethune-Cookman College and then after Bill finished, well, his parents asked him where did he want to go to school. He said, "Well, I want to go to Bethune-Cookman College because Jim Hair went there."

Well, Bill Beckner became the first black lawyer in the town and stayed well there in all kinds of adverse situations. But Bill did an outstanding job, outstanding job. We still get together today. We have terrific discussions; we share books together; we are great admirers of Nora Neale Hurston, one of the great black writers, the first woman, black woman to finish Barnard College up here. Her story's well known. But she taught at Lincoln Park Academy once—not during our time. But Bill and I really admire her too as another person—she had books on things like that. The last time I was down there, we went out to visit her grave.* It's the only grave I found in the cemetery with a tombstone on it, which was placed there recently by Alice Walker, who also admired Thurston.

Bill and I have shared many wonderful experiences together. He's a terrific guy. He's old now. He's retired and he's disabled really. In fact, the governor about two years ago invited him to a special program when they were celebrating Black History Month, as one of the leaders in Florida over the years.

So when it comes to talking about figures, I could go on for days and days because I've got many of them who were that way. My Sunday school superintendent and teacher there was Gerald Warwick, an outstanding guy, really. I mean, these are really positive figures.

---

* After her death in January 1960, Hurston, who was in financial difficulty, was buried in an unmarked grave in the Garden of Heavenly Rest cemetery in Fort Pierce, Florida. In 1973 African American novelist Alice Walker and scholar Charlotte Hunt placed a marker for Hurston in the cemetery.

One of the most unusual presence I've ever seen as one of my leaders was a fellow by the name of Jim Kennedy who lived in a town nearby. We all called him Captain Jim. Jim Kennedy was unusual in the sense that in this town there were killings every week. All you had to do was go to one of these, say, rough spots—your pool halls, or your bars, where they would gamble and so forth.

Paul Stillwell: Is this in Fort Pierce you're talking about?

Mr. Hair: Right. And every week, every weekend there was like two or three people getting killed, shot, cut to death, or whatever. Well, what made Jim Kennedy so unusual was he had this poolroom and barbershop there. And the man never had a fight, a gunshot, anything in that poolroom. Never once. But it was because of Jim Kennedy.

Paul Stillwell: What was it about him that prevented that?

Mr. Hair: It was the man and what he stood for, and what he meant to those people. He was one of the most decent individuals you could find. A man of integrity, a man of honesty. He was the sort of guy who was never above anyone else. He never had a condescending attitude toward anyone. I can remember that after his poolroom closed at 12:00 on Saturday night because of the curfew law, he would then take the whole group—four or five trucks, maybe—and he'd go out to this place called Humdinger. It was right outside the county line. They'd continue gambling, but if they had disagreements on things, enough to kill another person, whoever it was, they said, "Wait now. Let's get the captain." And the captain would come in and settle the thing.

Paul Stillwell: Sounds like he should have been a judge.

Mr. Hair: Oh, he should—I'm telling you. But his skills at dealing with people, and listening to them, and talking with them, he taught me more about that than I learned, say, in the school's social service getting my master's degree. He taught me that skill, more about it. I never got up to him. But he was just a great type of individual. So, as I say, there are many outstanding people that I met in my life.

Paul Stillwell: Well, I think I perhaps interrupted you in your list on the Golden Thirteen members.

Mr. Hair: Yes, right. Right.

I think I finished with Cooper. The only other one was Sublett. Now Sublett, again, was more of the quiet, listener-type person in the group but obviously anxious to learn and anxious to be a part of the group, and so forth. But I don't remember him contributing too much to the group except, as I stated, in listening and being a part of the group, and that sort of thing. Of course, I'm sure he contributed wherever he could in those discussions. But he was a wonderful person there in the group, and we all got together and really stuck together, and really admired each other there.

Paul Stillwell: Well, Sublett is an extremely friendly person.

Mr. Hair: Yes, he is. He really is, a very friendly person. He's another one that I receive correspondence from now quite a bit too.

Paul Stillwell: Well, you showed me that photo from Mr. Van Ness in 1938, and on the back he spelled your name H-A-I-R. It's now spelled H-A-I-R. But in the middle, in your Navy time, it was H-A-R-E, so I'd appreciate it if you could explain that.

Mr. Hair: Yes. Okay, very good, very good.

Following the death of my parents—my father first when I was about eight, and then my mother—I was working with this family and they kept insisting with me that I should not spell my name H-A-I-R, which is the correct way to spell it. But I should spell it H-A-R-E. Through their persistence, for whatever reason, and working for them at that time, it really meant something in terms of what they were trying to do. Jobs were very difficult to get in those days. But they kept insisting on that. So from that I started spelling it H-A-R-E. I just put it down. It wasn't something done legally, or anything of that nature. And so that's how that H-A-R-E happened to get in there.

Paul Stillwell: About what year would you say that was?

Mr. Hair: That must have been about 1935-36. Just before I went to college that's how I remember that.

Paul Stillwell: Who was the family?

Mr. Hair: The Brown family, the Browns.

Paul Stillwell: Where were there?

Mr. Hair: Frank Brown. They were there in Fort Pierce. And at that time I was working for them in a drugstore there.

Paul Stillwell: Well, it's interesting then, that's three years later Van Ness is still spelling it the correct way.

Mr. Hair: Yes.

Paul Stillwell: So did you sometimes use one in one situation and the other in another?

Mr. Hair: Well, I used H-A-I-R there most of the time. But at that time I spelled it that way. I put it on one of the school papers, and then it got into my school record as H-A-R-E after high school. Not in my high school but after. When I first went to college it got H-A-I-R, and that's the way it was. And then when my transcript was transferred and then it was H-A-R-E and that's when it got started, first year of college.

Paul Stillwell: And it was picked up H-A-R-E in the Navy as well.

Mr. Hair: Yes, right. That's correct. Because I had to have my transcript and all that for the Navy. So that's why that was spelled that way.

Paul Stillwell: When did you go back then to H-A-I-R?

Mr. Hair: I guess about the only time I really used that was mainly through college. I don't remember the specific date that I went back to H-A-I-R, but it was mainly through college that I spelled it H-A-R-E. And after that it was H-A-I-R. In fact, I was married H-A-I-R in 1947.

Paul Stillwell: Well, you may have kept it H-A-R-E through the Navy . . .

Mr. Hair: Through the college and Navy, and then after that I used H-A-I-R. In fact, after that, I notified the Navy because I got a GI mortgage on my house when I bought my house. I signed affidavits to the effect then that my name was H-A-I-R and that H-A-I-R and H-A-R-E was one in the same person. I had to sign that affidavit so I could get it right on my mortgage.

Paul Stillwell: But that created some confusion then getting you back with the Golden Thirteen years later.

Mr. Hair: Yes, yes. It did. It did, right.

Paul Stillwell: Interesting the ramifications that come from working for some people in a drugstore.

Mr. Hair: Yes, yes, that's right.

Paul Stillwell: And you don't remember what their reason was?

Mr. Hair: Oh, now that I look back on it, I didn't understand it too much at that time. The reason was the Browns were the type of persons who really wanted to be white. Their identification was with white, which I didn't quite understand at that time, but I was into tennis. I was into all sports, but tennis mainly. There was this white tennis player by the name of Hare. I've forgotten his first name. So they always used that. They said, "Look, now the correct way to spell it is the way he spells it." They kept persisting in this, and that's how this really got started. But I think it was really because they did not identify with blacks very much. I think that was their basic reason for it.

It's a sad thing with that family because they did very well there. They had seven children there, orange groves and things of that nature. And today they have nothing. Their kids went every direction, and each one was sort of self-destructive.

Paul Stillwell: It's unfortunate.

Mr. Hair: It really was, it really was with that family.

Paul Stillwell: We were talking about that atmosphere in your training period. What was the attitude of the instructors toward you as a group of students? Did you think they were honestly trying to help you learn?

Mr. Hair: Well, I wouldn't generalize in terms of all the instructors there. But my impression for most of the instructors was that they were there because they had to perform a duty. Not that they cared anything about us. They came across to me in that sense of just being there to carry out their job. This was a job they had assigned to them, and they were going to do it for that reason, not that they were interested in whether we passed or not. In fact, at the completion of it, one of them confessed to us that he came there under protest. But he admitted that after we were doing so well, he sort of changed, had a change of heart then, so to speak. But, no, they didn't impress me as really being there out of interest in really seeing us achieve, or something like that. In fact, this guy thought that he was going to flunk us. But fortunately, we were able to circumvent that.

Paul Stillwell: Sounds as if perhaps he wanted to flunk you.

Mr. Hair: Yes. Well, he admitted that he came here with that idea, that he was going to flunk us. But after we were doing so well, then he sort of changed his mind.

Paul Stillwell: Did the instructors, in general, have a condescending attitude?

Mr. Hair: Oh, yes. I would say so.

Paul Stillwell: How did they come across?

Mr. Hair: Well, well, it's just something that you can feel. When they're teaching you, it comes across as sort of cold, indifferent sort of thing, that they figure this Navy regs and whatnot and such and such and such, you know. And you go on and on and on with that. But it didn't come across with any kind of sensitivity feelings of wanting you to succeed or anything of that nature. Now, none of them would come out and say, "Look, this and this is the case, and the heck with you," or that sort of thing. There was no "Get it or get out," or something like that. None of them would say that, but it was just a feeling that they portrayed at that time. And there's something to say, there's something definite put forth. But I couldn't say it about all of them. I think a few of them were sincere, and they were there to see that you got what they were teaching.

Paul Stillwell: Certainly put John Dille in that category.

Mr. Hair: Oh, yes, John Dille was in that category. Right.

Paul Stillwell: How was he different? What do you remember specifically about him?

Mr. Hair: I think John Dille sort of portrayed to the class that he was a military man, and he was there to see that you got it, to see that you learned. He brought many things to the class in his attitude toward us that he was not only there to teach but to see that you get it.

And to do this, and to do that, and the other thing. But still in a very professional fashion. He wasn't going to . . .

Paul Stillwell: He wouldn't have bent the rules.

Mr. Hair: He wouldn't have bent the rules at all, no, which I thought was very good too. But John Dille was that type of person.

I'll never forget the delight that I had in one of his classes when he came in, and he was sharing with us at one time about the progress of the war. Up to this point, we had been on the defensive. And in this class he came in—I've forgotten the specific battle now—but it was a battle where, for the first time here where we went on the offensive. And he was pointing this out and what this meant. We got to get these things [unclear]. It was that sort of thing; you got a good feeling about it. That here's a guy here that's not only interested in our country, but he's interested in getting this class going here. It was that sort of thing.

Paul Stillwell: It could have been the invasion of the Marshall Islands. That was in February of '44.

Mr. Hair: Yes, it might have been that. It might have been that. Yes, think it was; I think it was.

Paul Stillwell: Did you feel a sense of personal warmth from him?

Mr. Hair: I tell you, we were so busy there in subject matter, so I don't know if I could call it personal warmth. I don't think I could, but I think I felt a sincerity about John Dille, the man, the professional man that was here to do a job. I just got the feeling, "Here's a good military man here, and he's out to see that we get it." And that was it. You know what I mean? He didn't ever show any favors or anything but "Doggone, let's get this." It was a military thing. That's the way I felt about John Dille.

Paul Stillwell: I guess you had at least one black instructor too.

Mr. Hair: Yes.

Paul Stillwell: Do you remember him?

Mr. Hair: Yes, right. Right, yes. He was the one who, I think, taught us math. Was his name Payton or something like that?

Paul Stillwell: Noble Payton.*

Mr. Hair: Yes, right.

Now, he was the type of guy in the mold of John Dille. He came in there to carry out an assigned task, and he did it. And we could have used the situation with him because he's black: "Now you know he's going to be good to us," and so forth and so on. No, Payton didn't get into that sort of thing. He taught, and we followed instructions. He was very helpful; he was very helpful. Like John Dille, he was determined that you get the subject matter.

Paul Stillwell: Was he a civilian?

Mr. Hair: No, no. I'm pretty sure he was a chief petty officer. They were wonderful guys, both of them.

Paul Stillwell: He would certainly have no reason to impede you.

Mr. Hair: No, no, no. That's true. That's true, he wouldn't. But my point is, see, you might get a person of any color. Could be black person, white person who might try to impede you. See what I mean? But what I'm talking about here is the quality that these people demonstrated in the classroom. He and Jack Dille were those types of people.

---

* Before entering the Navy, Noble F. Payton had taught chemistry and physics at Hampton Institute.

Paul Stillwell: You wonder if Commander Armstrong was frightened by this sort of thing, and he had to have Goodwin coming to him to sort of give him some security on it.

Mr. Hair: Yes, yes, yes. I think so. I think he may have been insecure in his position there at that time, because he'd been brought in as an expert on Negro affairs, so to speak. He had his history in terms of education at Hampton and so forth.* His father before him and so forth. But, anyway, it was obvious that he needed some kind of go-between there, and Goodwin served that role. And while I personally wouldn't like that sort of thing, I must admit that I think that Goodwin did quite an excellent job in that role, because Armstrong really needed it.

Paul Stillwell: Did you or any of the group have any sense of resentment toward Goodwin for doing that?

Mr. Hair: Oh, I'm sure there was some. Yes, there was some. I can remember the time that I resented certain things, but Goodwin was in such a position that you had to keep your resentment to yourself. I know I was aware of it, and I believe the rest of the guys in the group there were aware of it.

Paul Stillwell: He could be sort of a tattletale.

Mr. Hair: Oh, he could. He could. He could really hurt us. He could have, and we weren't about ready to let him do that. And on that same thing, I think this was reflected on the group throughout. Because we had all kinds of situations where we could have been hurt. But we had to, so to speak, maintain our control and keep our goal in mind. Because anything could have toppled this whole project right away. So we had to really take a lot of stuff at that time, in order to accomplish our goal that we started out for. So, along with Goodwin, we had other situations. Goodwin was right there as a member of the group, which made us more sensitive to this situation.

---

* Commander Daniel Armstrong's father, Brigadier General Samuel Chapman Armstrong (1839-1893), was colonel of a black regiment in the Civil War. That led to his interest in vocational education for black students. In 1868 he founded the Hampton Normal and Agricultural Institute at Hampton, Virginia.

Paul Stillwell: Was it easier to relax when he wasn't around?

Mr. Hair: Oh, yes. Oh, yes. In fact, that's when we started playing a little dice.

Imagine being there in that barracks all that time and not being able to get out, and just study, study, study, morning to night. And you visit all the time, which was great. We didn't mind that. But felt like we needed a little relaxation or something, and I'm pretty sure it was me who said, "Let's shoot some dice or something." Somebody had some dice on them. And we started playing for pennies or something like that. But that's when he came by with the [unclear] and saw us there. And like a big general, he stood up, "Up, men! We will not have that as officers of the United States Navy. No." And he meant it, and we knew he meant it. And we straightened up.

Paul Stillwell: Did you get any opportunities for liberty while you were in that training?

Mr. Hair: No, none whatsoever. None.

Paul Stillwell: Well, it sounds like there'd be a lot of potential there to get on each other's nerves.

Mr. Hair: Oh, there was, no doubt about it. No doubt about it. But, you see, this was compensated due to our intensive studying and activities. Then we had others in the group there who were great. Like Jesse was never at a loss for words. Jesse had an outstanding sense of humor. He was great. We had guys like that. And there were guys that would chip in once in a while who could make you laugh about something to break all this tension and whatnot. If a guy was getting up tight, somebody would talk to him, like old Dalton Baugh did. I guess he was one of the more mature guys. You couldn't raise a hair on him. He was always in a [unclear]. "Quiet down," and so forth. He was great. And Jesse and Graham and the rest of them were some really levelheaded guys. A few of them were really levelheaded and could help to alleviate some of the tension we had there. It was great.

Mr. James E. Hair, Interview #2 (11/10/88) – Page 145

Paul Stillwell: Did you have other forms of recreation or amusement within the barracks?

Mr. Hair: No. There was no recreation or amusement there. Our amusement was study. As I said, at night we would put our blankets up to the windows in the head there and go in there studying. We did that so we couldn't be seen from outside, because we were supposed to be in bed, but in a few times, other things we hadn't completed, we'd do it that way.

Paul Stillwell: Did you feel a lot of pressure that you were representing tens of thousands of other navy men?

Mr. Hair: No, I didn't feel that at that time. I really didn't. I was very much aware of the fact that we were going to this school and this was the first school that had been made known to us by Armstrong and some of the others there. But I never really felt that way. No, I saw it mainly as a job we had to do for the Navy at that time, and that was it.

Paul Stillwell: Was there any limitation on what you could communicate with friends or relatives about what you were doing?

Mr. Hair: Oh, yes, there was. We were always taught to be very careful of what we would say about what we were doing. So we were always aware of that. I never told anyone about what I was doing there in Officer Candidate School. In fact, my relatives and all didn't know about it until after it was over with. That was because of Navy policy in those days where you just didn't go out and blab. What do you say, "Loose tongues sink a ship," or something like that?

So you were always aware of that, and you didn't want to do anything that would upset the Navy plans in any way. So I really never told anyone about it.

Paul Stillwell: Well, and the fact that they had you kept apart by yourself limited a lot of your opportunity to do that.

Mr. Hair: Right. And come to think of it, I don't know if I even wrote any letters during that time. I can't recall having written any letters then.

Paul Stillwell: Do you remember if you were discouraged from doing so?

Mr. Hair: I don't remember that specifically, in that sense of not writing any letters. But I do remember being told specifically that—I think someone did say, "Don't tell anyone about this class." That sort of thing. They didn't tell us we couldn't write letters, but I don't recall having written any letters during that time.

Paul Stillwell: What do you remember about getting out of the barracks for physical exercise or that sort of thing?

Mr. Hair: Yes, we used to go out for physical exercises over in the gym. And for swimming, and occasionally, take ourselves over there for courses in lifesaving and stuff like that. But that was all done right in the gym. We would go for exercise and whatnot.

Paul Stillwell: That would be a great break from all the study, study, study.

Mr. Hair: Yes. And that would help to relieve the tension a lot, too, that we had there. That was great. I was always glad to do that whenever we could get over there, but we didn't do much swimming for exercise. Most of the swimming was for lifesavers. Sometimes you jumped in the water to save someone. It was a class. So that was our main thing there.

Paul Stillwell: That was the thing that Cooper hurt his back on.[*]

Mr. Hair: Oh, yes.

Paul Stillwell: Somebody had left a bar of soap on the diving board.

---

[*] See the Naval Institute oral history of George C. Cooper.

Mr. Hair: I don't remember that. I remember sometime after Cooper wrote me once about something like that, but I couldn't remember that incident though.

Paul Stillwell: He said that's what kept him from going overseas.

Mr. Hair: Oh? Because I thought he was just trying to hide. Being an old salt, I used to tell all of them, "All you guys are afraid to go to sea."

Paul Stillwell: I think Arbor really wanted to.

Mr. Hair: Oh, yes. I think Jesse would have gone, because he had gone to quartermaster school, and he really wanted to go to sea. I know John Reagan often talked about it, but I don't know how much John Reagan wanted to get out there. But I know Jesse would have gone. I'll tell you another one, Dalton Baugh, would have gone, too. Dalton Baugh, no question about it. Dalton Baugh would have gone. But many others there, but I just can't think of them right now.

Paul Stillwell: Did you also have some experience in giving orders to the boots while you were in officer training?

Mr. Hair: No, no, we didn't.
  The only time we had any connection with the boots, as I recall, was, as I say to go over the term in a class to be a lifesaver. When they brought all these guys, and then they'd jump and those who couldn't swim, you had to get down there and get them out. That's the only connection I can recall with anyone in boots. The rest of the time was mainly study, study, study, study. Yes. It was a very intensified program there, very much so.

Paul Stillwell: Are there any of the specific subjects that stand out in your mind?

Mr. Hair: Oh, I used to love Navy regs; I used to love Navy law and justice and stuff like that. I used to love that aspect of it. Yes. That was the real, real good, good course there. And it really brought a lot of debates and whatnot. Discussing different cases and Navy procedures and policies and things of that nature. That I remember was very good. Of course, all the others were very interesting. I guess the reason I enjoyed that was because later on went on to school at Naval Law and Justice out at Port Hueneme, California, which was great, because we could get into a lot of debates there on different cases and things of that nature. Plus I served once or twice on a few cases out in the Pacific, things of that nature.

Paul Stillwell: Any of those cases you especially remember?

Mr. Hair: I remember one case we had there where we brought this guy up on charges of sitting on a bunk bed of another sailor. He was accused of pulling the other guy's chain. No, it was one of those cases. We had that case there aboard ship, which went on for quite some time. The guy in the case who'd chosen me was quite an actor, and I used it in the case. Somehow or another, we got tangled up in some legal Navy regs there on some question there. The time ran out on the case, so it was just thrown out.

Paul Stillwell: How were you using his ability as an actor?

Mr. Hair: Well, to get him to not answer questions. He could go through all these different gyrations and all motions, and all this, and pretend he didn't understand the question. But at the same time, doing it in a real funny way. The guy even had me laughing up there at times. Of course, I couldn't show it right there. I had to be serious. But it was things like that, and it kept dragging the case out. Our purpose was to drag the case out until the deadline, and we were successful in it.

Paul Stillwell: Just from a completely detached viewpoint, that seemed pretty petty, sitting on somebody else's bunk.

Mr. Hair: Yes, yes. That's right, that's right. But the Navy had a law at that time about that.

Paul Stillwell: Well, they're very particular. A lot of these things stem from old traditions too.

Mr. Hair: Yes, yes. That's right, but that was the law then, and that's why that happened.

Paul Stillwell: It sounds as if Lear really fell in with those traditions and customs.

Mr. Hair: Oh, yes, he really did.

Paul Stillwell: Did you enjoy that aspect of the Navy?

Mr. Hair: No, I really couldn't say that I enjoyed it, but at the same time I knew that this was a part of Navy law and justice. Having completed this school there, I knew I was there to uphold this law. But as I say, like with this guy, the thing that tripped him was that there was an old thing in the Navy regs when you couldn't get a person to talk—you know how big and thick that Navy reg is—was that in order for the prosecutor to proceed—I've forgotten just the exact words, but it was something to the effect that, "The man stood mum, and I will proceed." But that had to be there in those old navy regs. But this guy didn't know that. So this is what we used, or gambled on, until the time ran out. But in the meantime, this guy was putting on quite an act, which was really a point of his defense.

Paul Stillwell: You talked about this investigation that went on about the various members of the officer group, perhaps the FBI doing it. What were your own feelings about that? Did you resent the fact that you were investigated?

Mr. Hair: No, I didn't resent it at that time. Not at all, because, again, I'm looking back at the time then. This was a new experiment the Navy was having, and they felt then that they had to get someone that they were sure of, that was qualified, and could meet the necessary standards and things of that nature. But at that time, I didn't have any particular feeling. Let me put it this way: I just accepted at that time that this was a part of reality. This was the thing that was happening throughout then, and I couldn't do a thing about it. I felt that that if I were to jump up now and complain about this, it was going to really hurt me at that particular time. So in that sense, I just didn't think too much about it.

Paul Stillwell: On the other hand, if you'd come through an investigation and gotten a clean bill of health, then you've got an endorsement that somebody doesn't have who hasn't been investigated.

Mr. Hair: Yes, that's right. Another thing then, too, you see in those days it was a part of our society there that in order to get a job—in fact, I've still got letters now from the 1930s from this church, or from this teacher, or from this professor, whatever, recommending me for a job. Giving me a clean bill of health. That was our thing in those days, just to get any kind of a job. You had to have a reference letter or something, even if it was for dishwasher only. You know what I mean? I've still got some of those old letters today.

Paul Stillwell: What evidence did you have of how thorough the investigation was in your case?

Mr. Hair: Well, one was from the Peacocks, the people that I worked for at one time as a chauffeur and a butler, and they told me about it afterward. I never asked them; I never even had to ask them. They never had the need to tell me, because I knew what they would say about me. I felt just that comfortable with them. They were two wonderful, wonderful people in that day and age. They were really terrific. Yes, they really were.

Paul Stillwell: The exception to most employers, I take it.

Mr. Hair: Yes, yes, that's true. They really were, really were.

Paul Stillwell: I interviewed Mummy Williams this summer, and he said the investigation turned up that he had been involved in labor organizing.* He said Dille told him about that and that's the reason that he wasn't commissioned.

Mr. Hair: Yes. Right.

Paul Stillwell: How does that strike you?

Mr. Hair: That he was involved in labor?

Paul Stillwell: If that were a disqualifying thing, why do you think the Navy they would have even admitted him to the class?

Mr. Hair: I would think that they would not have admitted him to the class if that were the disqualifying thing. But on second thought, I really don't know. I really don't know, because we did a lot of weird things in those days. We really did; we did a lot of weird things. But it doesn't seem to make sense that if he was in organized labor that they would put him in the class. I don't see the logic in it, but, as I say, I really don't know.

Paul Stillwell: The Communist Party was making overtures to blacks in that era and that might have shown up in investigation.

Mr. Hair: Oh, yes, right.

---

* Lewis R. Williams was one of the three officer candidates who were not commissioned after the training course.

Paul Stillwell: Did you have any involvement in that? Did the Communist party ever approach you?

Mr. Hair: No, no, the Communist party never, never approached me. At least not that I ever knew of.

Interesting that you mention that though, because, see, so many of us were afraid of the Communists during that time. I didn't really become acquainted and gain much knowledge about the Communists until, really, after the war. And that was during the McCarthy days and things of that nature.[*] I remember once I picked up a newspaper on the subway. And I thought it was the *Daily News*, and I started reading it. And then all of a sudden I looked and it was the *Daily Worker*. Well, you should have seen me getting away from that thing. But it was out of fear for that sort of thing, because it was so rampant in those days.

Paul Stillwell: Well, I would say the fear was greater in the '50s than it was in the '30s.

Mr. Hair: Yes, yes, that's right. That's what I say—that I knew of the Communists, but I didn't know much about them at that time. Along that same line, for example, at Bethune-Cookman College, we used to have these speakers to come in for symposiums, seminars, and things of that nature. And I never will forget this; we had this speaker come in—this was in about 1938—and she was talking about Hitler.[†] She went on to talk about how this man is going to destroy the whole world, and so forth. I was thinking to myself, "Goodness, that guy must be crazy. Either that or the speaker is crazy," because at that time we were just getting to know.

But nothing then about Communists. That sort of came later with me.

---

[*] As a U.S. senator from Wisconsin in the early 1950s, Joseph R. McCarthy went on an anti-Communist witch hunt that came to be dubbed by the pejorative term "McCarthyism." He was eventually censured by the Senate.
[†] Adolf Hitler was Chancellor of Germany from 1933 until his death by suicide on 30 April 1945.

Mr. James E. Hair, Interview #2 (11/10/88) – Page 153

Paul Stillwell: Speaking of Hitler, I saw a documentary on television last night—that last night was the 50th anniversary of the Kristallnacht when they burned a thousand synagogues and broke windows.* That really was the beginning of the holocaust.

Mr. Hair: Yes, yes.

I guess I always considered myself very fortunate to have had the parents that I had. I mention this because, you see, when I came up in South Carolina, we really had more physical integration there than probably the North has ever known. It was farm country where the black lived here and the white lived there, and so forth. The beautiful part about it you had communication between them. They speak, and, how's this one, how's that, and so forth. This communication always went on. But the reason why I mention this is because I grew up really not knowing anything about discrimination and racism in those days. I guess I was a teen before I really had my first experiences in that.

In my family my parents there never taught anything about racism, or being against another group, or all these slurs. I never saw heard, never saw that sort of thing in my life. Of course, we, 21 of us there, and I guess we were like a United Nations, every color imagined. But I mention this because I grew up with the qualification of not being able to distinguish what a person really is—what race he belongs to, nationality, or what. I just never could do that.

It was interesting after my experience on the USS *Mason*, and this is several years later after [unclear] and I had gotten together, long after the war was over, just a few years ago. As much as we'd been together, the question of Jews had never come up. I'm sure we had mentioned something about blacks—what the blacks think about the *Mason*, something like that trying to get his book together. I'd tell him. Anyway, this went on for quite a while, and then, eventually, one day—I'm trying to remember exactly how it happened but to sort of paraphrase it, somehow or other he asked me, "Do you know I'm Jewish?"

I said, "No, I didn't know that." And I actually didn't. Now we served aboard ship together and everything. That didn't ever come up with me. I didn't know what he

---

* Kristallnacht was an anti-Jewish attack in Germany and Austria on the night of 9-10 November 1938. The term translated as "Crystal Night" and also as "the night of the broken glass." The Nazi attacks resulted in the murders and arrests of many Jewish people and the destruction of a great deal of property.

was. I believed he was a white person as far as I'm concerned. You know what I mean? That's, that's the only thing I knew, and sometimes I wasn't too sure about that because I remember when I was in New Orleans I had trouble distinguishing who was white and who was black. But that's what I mean by my qualification in that field. I've met people who swear they can just look at somebody and tell right away what he is. They usually look at the hair on his arms, and so forth, you can tell about that. There's all these different things.

But, anyway, I thank God I never, I never had that qualification. I just never needed it.

Paul Stillwell: Wesley Brown said one of the amazing things to him when he went to the Naval Academy was to learn that there were other kinds of prejudice besides anti-black.[*]

Mr. Hair: Yes, right. Right, yes, that's true. That really does. It really does happen. But, thank God, I never really got into that. I really never got into that.

Paul Stillwell: Looking back again to the 1930s, there were a number of stereotypes for blacks: Stepin Fetchit, and Amos 'n' Andy, and so forth.[†] What was your view of those at the time? Were you bothered by them? Did you accept them?

Mr. Hair: Oh, I thought they were very funny. I thought they were very funny at that time. I guess my main thing was then was just to look at it as another show and that it was something funny, and that was it.

I guess deep down inside I never cared too much with the stereotype, say, the Stepin Fetchit, things of that nature. But I must say that I really enjoyed some of the talk shows, and whatnot, but you understand, I can't remember some of the specifics of them

---

[*] Ensign Wesley A. Brown, USN, became the first black graduate of the Naval Academy in 1949, then entered the Civil Engineer Corps. He retired as a lieutenant commander in 1969. His oral history is in the Naval Institute collection.

[†] Stepin Fetchit was the stage name of black actor/comedian Lincoln Theodore Monroe Andrew Perry (1902-1985). He played characters who acted obsequiously toward whites. "Amos 'n' Andy" was a radio comedy program in which two white actors played black characters.

now. But, as I say, I just saw him as being funny in something, but that was about it. That was about the best he could do at that time. It was one of those things.

Paul Stillwell: The real irony is that the actors portraying Amos and Andy were white.

Mr. Hair: Yes, that's right, that's right. That's right. And where'd I read someplace recently where they were trying to make a comeback or something on that show?

Paul Stillwell: Oh, I didn't hear that.

Mr. Hair: Yes, someplace I read that recently.

Paul Stillwell: What role or importance would you ascribe to the success of Joe Louis in the 1930s?

Mr. Hair: Joe Louis was, first of all, just an outstanding boxer. Joe was limited in terms of the real world, in terms of how to manage.* I guess he had no real education in that area, so he was limited. I think that Joe just relied on Mike Jacobs there that he was going to do right by him, sort of a carryover from the slavery days that your master's going to take care of you.† I think he was influenced by that. It was a very unfortunate thing. But as an individual, Joe Louis was really a jewel. He was really a peach of a guy. Was really good. I had an opportunity to be with him on a few occasions, you know. In fact, I was invited to a party that he gave in the Theresa Hotel down on 125th Street. Of course, at the end of the party, he called Mike Jacobs to tell him what the deal was, send a check or something like that. But Joe Louis was a jewel of a man, though, he really was. I think I told you about the time that he and I were in a contest for the same girl.

Paul Stillwell: I didn't recall that, no.

---

* Louis wound up in serious difficulty with the Internal Revenue Service over tax liabilities.
† Michael S. Jacobs was a prominent boxing promoter who had a major role in shaping Louis's career.

Mr. Hair: This was when I was skipper of the tug here. When I got a chance to be off, occasionally I would come to the Theresa Hotel. Well, Joe was usually always there. It was there at the hotel, in the lounge there or something, where I saw this beautiful gal. I went over some way or another and introduced myself and tried to make an impression on her, which I thought I had. So we were going out to dinner that night. Well, anyway, she and her mother were staying at the Theresa. So I went by to get her to find that Joe Louis was there. So right away I figured, "Well, I ought to really challenge Joe Louis, to show her that I'm not afraid of him. I don't care if he is a boxer." But Joe knew me; I met him in the hotel there, but we didn't know one another very closely. I went in and told her I was ready to take her out and then she started hesitating, saying, well, there was Joe there. I could see that, well, I couldn't compete with Joe in those days. And so, anyway, I jumped up and I said, "Well, what in the heck is this?" I told Joe, "You're not taking [I've forgotten her name, Mary, or whatever name it was] her out. She's my date for tonight. I'm taking her out."

He said, "No, you're not either." So I pulled off my jacket. I challenged him to a duel because I knew darn well he wasn't going to hit me. Well, I was trying to impress her, but it didn't make any impression on her. She still went out with Joe Louis. But that Joe was a heck of a wonderful guy, though, he really was—a great guy.

Paul Stillwell: Well, what was important about him is that in so many other areas of society, arbitrary rules could be made so that the competition would be unfair for blacks. But they couldn't do that in the ring.

Mr. Hair: Yes, right.

Paul Stillwell: He got to compete on his own merits.

Mr. Hair: Yes, he certainly did. He certainly did. He was a great guy, great guy.

You know, speaking about that sort of thing where Joe Louis ended up with no money, recently I was shocked. I was talking with a doctor whom I have a lot of faith in, a doctor in the field of education in the area of sociology, and whatnot, an older person. I was talking about Dr. Mary McLeod Bethune. We went on to talk about all the wonderful work she did and so forth, and then she shocked me by saying, "But, you know, she never got paid for it. It was all volunteer." And I didn't know that. So I bring this out in terms of what we're talking about with Joe Louis here, where we saw a lot of that. I guess we could go back to slavery, and whatnot, where we saw that where you slaved and you worked, but you didn't come to the point where you, say, as Bill Cosby said the other day where you struck a little vein and decided to mount it some place.[*] But that was a part of our history then.

Paul Stillwell: She had to support herself somehow.

Mr. Hair: Well, she was president of the school at that time. And she had many other positions, but I understand that her work with the government was a volunteer thing.

Paul Stillwell: Well, I'm sure she got a reward in terms of satisfaction that she was able to bring about so much good.

Mr. Hair: Oh, no doubt about it, no doubt about it. The epitaph on her tombstone is something to the effect that, "I gave of my life so that others could have life and have it more abundantly."

Paul Stillwell: That's a good one to have.

Mr. Hair: Yes, which is really great, really great. She was really a great person, great person—both of them, she and Joe Louis. Really great.

---

[*] William H. Cosby Jr. is a prominent black comedian and actor. He starred in the popular television sitcom "The Cosby Show" from 1984 to 1992.

Mr. James E. Hair, Interview #2 (11/10/88) – Page 158

Paul Stillwell: Well, there's certainly not an epitaph for the Golden Thirteen, because you're very much alive, but you've got a monument in that center up at Great Lakes, the in-processing center.*

Mr. Hair: Yes.

Paul Stillwell: How do you feel about having something like that as such a tangible memorial?

Mr. Hair: I think that's a great thing there, after having gone through so much. I still like to pinch myself that it's really there, that that has really happened. So I'm saying to myself, "Did I really go out there to Great Lakes for that? Did that really happen?" Then I think about the wonderful speech that Judge White gave out there that day, which was terrific. He was talking about the pursuit of happiness and that all people are created equal. Maybe this is an outgrowth of that at this time for this building to be dedicated to us there on that day. I think it's just a wonderful thing, and I think it's in a way showing that we are still growing, we're still growing and still in pursuit of that happiness and the recognition of the fact that all men are created equal. We have a goal and something to attain. It's really a wonderful thing, and I'm very proud of it.

Paul Stillwell: With good reason.

Mr. Hair: Yes, absolutely, absolutely.

Paul Stillwell: Well, and partly, it's a matter of luck, too, that you happened to be one of the ones. But, beyond that, it's a tribute to your efforts that you succeeded once you got the opportunity.

---

* On 5 June 1987, at the Great Lakes Naval Training Center, where the Golden Thirteen received their officer training in 1944, the Navy dedicated a new building named for the group. It is used for the in-processing of new recruits.

Mr. Hair: Yes, yes, that's right. We did. We succeeded, and in addition to that, the other thing that I look at when we see things like this, is that while we succeeded, we achieved what we were put there to do. I am forever grateful to the many people who made this possible. It was people like many of the different black churches, NAACP, A. Philip Randolph, and the sleeping car porters, and Dr. Mary McCloud Bethune, and many of the other Van Nesses, and so forth. They stood up for these sorts of things to change this closed enlistment policy to make it an open enlistment. Because without those, see, we never would have had this opportunity. So we just did what they told us to do after we were there to achieve this, and at the same time, I cannot help but think about the many hundreds of other guys who could have done the same thing that we did. So, in that sense, the good Lord was just with us. The good Lord was really with us. I'm forever grateful.

Paul Stillwell: Well, it was a matter of timing, also, that you were at the right age when the opportunity came along.

Mr. Hair: Yes, yes, that's true. That's really true, and you can go back to even thank my parents, because they had a hand in it.

Paul Stillwell: They certainly did.

Mr. Hair: And a brother there of mine who is really great, I'm telling you. I've got some wonderful sisters and brothers.

Paul Stillwell: Is this your brother Sam you're speaking of?

Mr. Hair: Yes, yes.

Paul Stillwell: What do you remember about him specifically?

Mr. Hair: Well, in terms of this achievement, you see, my brother Sam used to go down to [unclear]—the guy has really got a heart of gold in him because it started way back. First, there he was, he had his family, and so forth, but he paid for my mother's funeral. He paid for my brother's children's funeral in South Carolina. He paid for my brother's funeral in South Carolina. I couldn't begin to enumerate the many things that that guy has done, but personally, when I was up at Bethune-Cookman College, he paid for much of my education by fixing their cars for the college, and they let it go to the cost of my education. You know what I mean? He's that type of guy. And here's the guy that got up off the floor after a nervous breakdown to go out and succeed.

So when you talk about being thankful, boy, I couldn't get to name all the people to be thankful for. Stuckey, you know, James Stuckey, the old chauffeur. Mildred and Arleigh Peacock. When I went to them and said, "Look, I don't have a job. I want to go to college. Come on." They didn't have to do these things. So, no, we've got a lot to be thankful for. I know I have. Yes, indeed.

Paul Stillwell: Well, we all do, as you say.

Mr. Hair: Yes, yes, that's right.

Paul Stillwell: Well, I put together some questions here just from going back to the first transcript. And one thing that you mentioned before but we didn't really follow up on is that you said you didn't know for a long time your actual birth date. How did you find that out?

Mr. Hair: Oh, yes. Through the Census Bureau.

Paul Stillwell: When did you check into that?

Mr. Hair: Oh, just before I retired in 1981, because up to that point I never felt the need to know my age. I really didn't. For example, when I went in the Navy, I just gave them a year that I thought was the approximate age that I was. Because, you see, at that point when I was born in South Carolina, they didn't record birth certificates. But before I retired I knew that I had to produce something in order to get my retirement. So a group of sisters and brothers got together, and we inquired of the Census Bureau. It came back and said, more or less in general, that when the census was taken in 1920 there was the child in the home of—a boy, or son, or something like that—in the home by the name of James who was four years of age, and that was it. So you just figure out then it was 1915 because the census was taken in January of 1920. So at that time I hadn't found out. But other than that, there was no need to know my age as far as I was concerned. We never had birthday celebrations or anything of that nature. There was no time for that.

Paul Stillwell: You had so many in the family they'd been going on all the time.

Mr. Hair: That's right, that's right.

Paul Stillwell: What was it like growing up in such a large family. Was it very competitive?

Mr. Hair: Oh, it was terrific. It was terrific. We had some competition there, some sibling rivalry and stuff of that nature, but nothing really out of the usual. It was a wonderful experience. We shared a lot, and we were always busy. We were brought up on the work ethic. From there you went to church, went to Sunday school and church, and things of that nature. So we always had to schedule. We always had something to do. Not a matter of not having something to do.

So I still say it was a wonderful experience, and I think it's further demonstrated today. All the survivors today are still very much in touch—I'd say at least on a monthly basis.

Paul Stillwell: You mentioned that you had for a while a goal of being able to pick 100 pounds of cotton. In what period of time was that? Was that for a day?

Mr. Hair: Oh, that was for a day, yes. Because in those days I can remember—this was after my father passed away. My mother was able to do it, pick 100 pounds of cotton. That was quite an achievement there, to be able to do that.

Paul Stillwell: Do you remember how old you were when you got to that goal?

Mr. Hair: Oh, I must have been about six or seven when I thought about it. But I never reached that goal. I never reached that; I was just dreaming of the day that I would do it, but I never reached that goal. I picked a little a little sackful or something like that, but I never reached 100 pounds. No.

Paul Stillwell: Because you got into other things, I take it.

Mr. Hair: Well, no, because after that we left South Carolina and moved to Florida. And there were other things there. We had like the tomato fields, the bean fields, pepper fields, oranges, and things of that nature. Then we had the shrimp boats and all. All that sort of stuff was going on. So there were other things, no cotton there.

Paul Stillwell: That was the day-care center in that period, go out and pick cotton.

Mr. Hair: Yes, yes, that's right. In that hot sun too. It was very hot.

Paul Stillwell: Why did your mother specifically choose Florida after your father died?

Mr. Hair: Because, mainly because there were other relatives there and that, I'm sure, influenced her greatly. Not only that just because there were relatives there, but at that time Florida was "booming." They were building, and there were many, many jobs available. But as far as blacks were concerned then, it was mainly in the domestic fields and things of that nature, or maybe ditch digging. And, of course, picking in the fields, and whatnot, and picking oranges.

Mr. James E. Hair, Interview #2 (11/10/88) – Page 163

Paul Stillwell: What do you recall about your days in elementary school? How good a student were you?

Mr. Hair: Oh, I used to love school; I used to love school. Now, I don't remember my grades or anything of that nature now, but as a student I loved school; I loved studying. I loved to satisfy my teacher. I really admired my teachers; I thought they were just wonderful and really beautiful people, just stuff like that. They were very good with you. They were very kind and very anxious for you to learn. I became, I guess, like an eager beaver when it comes to study, because, as I moved up, I remember them promoting me at half year, during mid-term. In fact, they did that twice, which really was very bad for me, because it put me out of my group. Socially the group wouldn't accept me. They were older than I was. Here was just a little runt, and they wouldn't accept me. So in that sense it sort of backfired and, in fact, at times I wouldn't attend class just to keep from having to be rejected by this class again. Fortunately through the help of teachers and whatnot, I finally worked through that. But I later let them know I didn't want to be up there with that other class. Finally somebody saw it, so it worked out all right eventually. But that held me back somewhat.

Paul Stillwell: Well, from my having come to know you, I see you as a person of great enthusiasm, and I can imagine you taking that enthusiasm to your schoolwork.

Mr. Hair: Oh, yes, yes. I loved it, though. I loved it. And not only just the schoolwork, but in all the extracurricular activities I used to like to get into, like we put on plays and things of that nature. You volunteered for parts in the plays. The only thing I didn't get into was the music group. I couldn't make a joyful noise.

But I loved all those things, all those other activities, and sports and things. I think I told you we built the first tennis court there on the school grounds. It was a terrific experience, and had some wonderful teachers there, really great teachers who were really interested.

Paul Stillwell: How well qualified would you say they were?

Mr. Hair: The teachers? I'd say they were quite qualified for that day and age, very much so. Not that I am any expert on the English language, but today when I see so many of these guys on the news programs, and so forth, and how they kill the King's English, I say, "Oh, my God. This is something we got back in high school." As I say, any time they get beyond the present and past tense, they're lost.

Paul Stillwell: Well, I think their main qualifications are they look good and they're halfway funny.

Mr. Hair: Well, maybe that's it. Maybe that's it.

But, but I think it was a reflection of our teachers there. We had some really, some good teachers. Some I didn't think too highly of, but that's another matter.

Paul Stillwell: They probably were not as well educated as today's teachers.

Mr. Hair: Oh, no doubt about it. No doubt about it. A lot of those teachers only had junior college degrees, I think. Yes, that's right. If you got someone with four, then they start moving up to four years, and so forth. But it wasn't until years later that they started getting people with a master's degree or something like that. That usually was a principal or somebody like that.

Paul Stillwell: How much did the teachers try to involve you in learning about current events?

Mr. Hair: Oh, very much so. In fact, we had a current events class every day. And we had to bring in news of the day, and so forth, and news of the week because the class was only one or two days a week or something like that.

But we had, we had a current events class, and we had to do it.

Paul Stillwell: What sort of a town was Blackville? How big?

Mr. Hair: Oh, about the size of a football.

No, I'm just kidding. It was a very small town. Well, I tell you, it was so small that this actually happened there. I think they've changed it now, but for years the police precinct was the public telephone booth. That's right. He would park his car there beside that in case he got a call. There were very few telephones in the town. The only one in the beginning that had a telephone there, as far as the blacks were concerned, was the undertaker. That was mainly for out-of-town calls, in case somebody died or something like that. But that's the way it was in the beginning. It was a very small town.

Paul Stillwell: Would you have a guess as to the population?

Mr. Hair: Back in those days I'd say maybe 800 or 900 people or something like that as a guess.

Paul Stillwell: So you could know a pretty large portion of the people in the town.

Mr. Hair: Oh, we knew most of the people there, yes, practically all of the people there.

As I say, at that time there were two Hair families in the town. One was white and one was black, and we knew them. We talked together and things of that nature. The mayor of the town, Pickling, lived right down the block from us.

Paul Stillwell: And you've told me you didn't experience any discrimination or racial prejudice there.

Mr. Hair: Yes, yes. I'm sure they had some, but I guess with my young age then, I wasn't aware of it or anything of that nature.

Paul Stillwell: Well, there may have been rules that you just took for granted without questioning.

Mr. Hair: Yes, maybe so. And not only that but the lifestyle, see, where you went to work every day, worked on the farm, and so forth. We had a farm there. And then after that you went to church, and so forth. But then you would see these people in passing. When you saw most of the people in the town was when you went shopping on Saturday. See, everyone was there. Black and white—everybody would shop. "Oh, hi. How you doing? How's the family?" You know, want to know something.

Paul Stillwell: Was it sort of a farm community?

Mr. Hair: Oh, yes, definitely a farm community.

Paul Stillwell: The sorts of businesses that support farmers. Probably a general store.

Mr. Hair: A general store.

Paul Stillwell: Barber shop.

Mr. Hair: Yes, and a little post office.

Paul Stillwell: They probably still had a blacksmith in those days too.

Mr. Hair: Yes, they still had the blacksmith there. And then they had the stable there, Brown stable there, where you get horses and things like that. I guess he sold them there or something like that. That was about it.

Paul Stillwell: It sounds as if you have pretty happy memories of that experience.

Mr. Hair: Oh, yes, I do. Yes, I do. That's the reason I go by there every year. I go by there every year just to see it.

Paul Stillwell: When you got to Florida, did you have the same enthusiasm for learning?

Mr. Hair: Oh, yes. Oh, yes. See, that's when I really developed it more there. It started in South Carolina, but I really developed it more in Florida there, because it was really a terrific thing to be able to go to school to learn. It was exciting, and as I mentioned Ronald Warrick before, was super Sunday school superintendent. Well, his wife was a teacher there and she was a music teachers. She wrote the first school song for the school. We had plays and we had sports. It was mainly basketball in the beginning.

Paul Stillwell: You mentioned the discussions that took place in the shoe shop. What were some of the topics of those?

Mr. Hair: We would discuss a lot of current events. For example, Roosevelt and his different programs, what was going on. And each person shared different ideas about it. Some would agree with him, and some people did not agree with him. They'd explain why. They thought this wasn't a good program. But one of the big topics there was usually always around education. How important he had a good education program and these sorts of things. And these discussions were made up of blacks and whites. They were usually older people, mostly from the black and white community. But there were a few of us younger fellows who were interested in this would come in on it.

I remember I went in, not initially because of the discussion but because the guy who owned the shoe shop there, Worrey, was a terrific fisherman. We knew after a while we could get him to take us fishing. This is how it really got started. Then I learned about these different discussions which were very interesting, and that was really great.

Paul Stillwell: Well, and you had from your brother-in-law Estes this love of the water, also.

Mr. Hair: Oh, yes. No doubt about it.

Paul Stillwell: Well, I guess we'd have to put him down as one of your heroes also.

Mr. Hair: Oh, no doubt about it. He was a strong individual, very strong person. He was a person that was just believed in everybody getting along, and everybody doing the right sort of thing, and not to tread on your fellow man's rights, and things of that nature. I can remember situations whereby, in those days we used to have the whites coming into the black community looking for black women as prostitutes. It didn't matter if she was a prostitute at all, just a black woman. And how he would treat them. He would treat them, "Oh, yeah, surely I've got some—come with me." Because they would stop under the light. Well, he didn't want them under his light. So he would take them away, lead them out like he was going toward a house some place. As soon as he got out the light, oh, he would tear right into them and beat them up something awful. These things just went on. So that's how they stopped that so they would never come back again.

Paul Stillwell: Well, I can understand that.

Mr. Hair: With that sort of thing. See.

Paul Stillwell: But I'm sure that would create a reputation for him too.

Mr. Hair: Oh, it, it probably did, but he didn't mind that. He knew what sort of reputation he had. And they knew that he just didn't tolerate certain things. And that was the type of life that he lived.

Paul Stillwell: Certainly you got some of your values from him.

Mr. Hair: Oh, yes, no doubt about it. No doubt about it.

Paul Stillwell: What were some of the subjects that you were strong in during your school years?

Mr. Hair: I would say history and sociology. I used to love math. I was not an outstanding student in math. I used to love it. It was a challenge because a lot of the problems may be presented me with a challenge to try to solve them. But it was great. That was also brought about by those teachers because I had a terrific math teacher. And I remember Bethune-Cookman College, I had a terrific teacher there and Colson and Day. Both were terrific. Colson later became president of Brown Community College there. Outstanding teachers.

Paul Stillwell: Well, they also can be a real inspiration for you.

Mr. Hair: Oh, yes. No doubt about it.

Paul Stillwell: Was there any emphasis on black history or black studies during either high school or college years?

Mr. Hair: I don't think we called it black history then. I'm thinking then about Bethune-Cookman College. But it was just history, for example, maybe American History or something of that nature. I've forgotten the exact title. But I don't recall it specifically as black history. But we had it on all of our black historians, George Washington, Frederick Douglass, and, Du Bois, and many of the others that we had during that date.[*] Many, oh, outstanding writers, Nathaniel [unclear] and many others who wrote what was then called the Negro National Anthem. And, of course, throughout the college there, we had huge portraits of all of these black leaders. Not only just black, we had some white leaders there, too, at that time, because she had an integrated school there. It was integrated in terms of its programs, and whatnot, and not in terms of student body.

Paul Stillwell: How do you mean integrated by programs?

Mr. Hair: With all of our programs, like on Sunday our programs, and so forth, the audience was all integrated. Usually about 50-50%: 50% black, 50% white.

---

[*] Frederick Douglass escaped from slavery and became a noted lecturer and writer. He was editor of an abolitionist newspaper and was later consulted by President Abraham Lincoln. Douglass served as U.S. Minister to Haiti, 1889-91. W. E. B. Du Bois (1868-1963) was a noted American author, historian, editor, and civil rights activist.

But, as I say, I don't remember specifically calling the course Negro. You wouldn't think to call it Negro History then or something like that. But we had a lot of that.

Paul Stillwell: But I take it there was not as much emphasis on it as there is today.

Mr. Hair: No, no. No, I guess you're right in the sense as we see it today throughout. But we studied black history at Bethune-Cookman College. We had that there, yes.

Paul Stillwell: Was an indirect byproduct of this the instilling of pride and dignity in being black?

Mr. Hair: I always felt that way about myself. I always knew what I was, and I was proud of that fact. I'll tell you one thing that happened at Bethune-Cookman College that did help to emphasize that fact was with Mrs. Bethune. Back in the '30s, see, she really started this thing about black is beautiful. Maybe not specifically in terms of that as being a program or anything. But she would always start all of her talks and all of her lectures, and whatnot, by greeting us, "Oh my, what beautiful black boys and black girls," and she'd go on about how beautiful you are. And she put it another way, "You know, in this day and age, we're moving more and more to the point where it seems as though more whites want to be black. So look at your beaches and everything. They can't get dark enough." Know what I mean? With the suntan and whatnot. She said, "And we are doing just the reverse, where we're going out to buy all the Magnolia Bleaching Cream to see if we can become white." She said, "But you're beautiful. You don't need that."

These were the things she used to talk about, which really emphasized what I already knew about myself. And especially having come from a drugstore where one of our big items that we sold in that day was Magnolia Bleaching Cream. Because there were a lot of blacks who wanted to be white.

Paul Stillwell: Did the stuff actually have any effect?

Mr. Hair: It did make you a little lighter. It would make you lighter in the face where you put it, but everything else was the same color. But it would bleach you. It was like a bleach, no doubt about it. Yes. That's right.

Paul Stillwell: Probably a hair-straightener, too.

Mr. Hair: Oh, yes, we had a lot of that. The guy who owned the drugstore made a lot of money on that, because he had a lot of that there. Everybody was trying to straighten his hair or what we used to call caulking in those days, and make it straight. Put that stuff in there with the lye and stuff in it would make anything straight.

But that was it, though. She did a tremendous job there with that.

Paul Stillwell: Well, it's good psychology considering what you were likely to hear from other sources.

Mr. Hair: Yes, right, right. No doubt about it.

Paul Stillwell: How would you describe yourself as an athlete? You've mentioned tennis and basketball. How good were you at each of those?

Mr. Hair: Well, in those days, before we got these big six- and seven-footers, we had a good team. As I say, we were the number-two team in the state of Florida then and, of course, by becoming that we went to the all-Southern tournament that was in Tuskegee, Alabama, then. So we had a good team. For myself I loved it; I loved athletics. When you were in good shape and could really move and play and do things, it was really terrific.

Paul Stillwell: Were you fast?

Mr. Hair: Yes. Small so you had to be fast out there, otherwise you'd get killed. But you had to be really quick in those days.

Of course, the game then was nothing like the game is today. No, we wouldn't have a chance out there the way they play that game today. We had a different thing. For example, we could only shoot a two-handed set shot. No one-handed shot, because you were off the team if you started that stuff.

Paul Stillwell: I think you were likely to shoot from farther away from the basket than today too.

Mr. Hair: Yes, that was true. And we had some guys who could hit it pretty good. Yes, really could. I played basketball in high school, and that's what helped me in college, because I also made the varsity team in college, at Bethune-Cookman College.

Paul Stillwell: It was surprising to me that so many of the Golden Thirteen were such good athletes, and maybe that wasn't an accident. Maybe that was one of the selection factors.

Mr. Hair: Yes, yes, probably was.

Paul Stillwell: Though not all were.

Mr. Hair: Yes, right.
Of course, that was another thing about the military, too, in boot training. You had to be some kind of good physical specimen to go through that kind of training.

Paul Stillwell: Well, too, other aspects of it are the competitiveness and the teamwork. Both of those are useful in the officer-type situation.

Mr. Hair: Yes. No doubt about it; no doubt about it. Yes.

Paul Stillwell: You talked about the trip that you made to Tuskegee and the incident in the garage. Are there other things you remember about the inconveniences involved in traveling? That is difficulty in getting meals, or places to sleep, or get a car?

Mr. Hair: Well, we couldn't get meals on the road. The only time you could get a meal on the road if you stopped in a town that was big enough to have a black restaurant. And there weren't many of those, because most of the people did their cooking at home. Or there were no restaurants available for us on the road that we knew of. Now occasionally, but we didn't use them very much. Oh, once or twice we may have used it where we would run into a white restaurant where they would serve you from a back door, like a sandwich or just something like that. But that was about the extent of it, so we did use that.

The other inconvenience, too, was you couldn't buy gas at any service station, so you had to be highly selective there in terms of where you went to buy your gas. So we were limited throughout in many of those areas. There were many incidents; I can't remember all of them now.

Paul Stillwell: Are there any that you remember specifically?

Mr. Hair: Well, I told you about the one with the garage. I remember that one very well, because the thing that stood out was with the principal there being so afraid, really. That really hit me. I recognize that in those days you had to stay low on certain things, but he was obsessed with fear, which really caused the white guy to react more negatively toward us, and that was the thing that got me.

Paul Stillwell: Made him more aggressive.

Mr. Hair: Yes. Absolutely, absolutely. About to get all of us killed there.

But those were the main things, because we avoided a lot of those things. For example, we would play Melbourne; we would play West Palm Beach; we would play

Fort Lauderdale, and other things. Now, before we would leave, we would make sure that for those distances, see, that we had all of our gas, everything we needed in that car.

Paul Stillwell: Would you carry extra gas in a can?

Mr. Hair: No, but we knew we could put enough in the tank to get us from Fort Pierce to Fort Lauderdale which was about 100 miles. Same thing with West Palm Beach. Same thing with Melbourne. So it was no stopping, see. You didn't stop unless your car broke down or something, and then you were in trouble. So that's the way we avoided a lot of it, by being prepared and getting all our necessary supplies before we left.

Paul Stillwell: Did you then go back home the same day so you didn't have to stay overnight?

Mr. Hair: No, usually we stayed overnight. What happened was that the parents of children in the school would take one or two of us in their homes to spend the night, see. Usually that's the way it would work out, except on maybe a short trip, now like sometimes we'd go and come back that same night. But most of the time the other schools supplied you with the accommodation for overnight.

Paul Stillwell: You talked about carrying the gun the time you went out fishing with Estes. Were guns readily available?

Mr. Hair: Oh, yes. Yes, this is one of the things that amaze me now about the topic of gun control. Because this was an accepted thing throughout the South. Everybody had a gun; there was no problem to get a gun. There was no problem.

I remember when I was a kid there in South Carolina growing up that we had a big type of a big dump yard or something over there. But this guy dealt in all kinds of iron works. I guess he would sell them or whatnot. Well, heck, I could go over there and find a gun.

Paul Stillwell: Somebody had just thrown away.

Mr. Hair: Yes, it was an old gun he figured was no good so he'd throw it away. But you'd get it, and it would work.

But that was an accepted thing. Every home had a gun because, the simple fact, not so much the protection of their homes, and so forth back then, not to keep anyone out or something. That may have been a minor factor, but the main thing they needed the guns for was hunting and whatnot. We did a lot of that. And not only that, but sometimes you'd have hawks that tried to get your chickens. And you had the guns there to protect yourself, protect your chickens and whatnot. It was anything like that.

Paul Stillwell: So these were rifles you carried rather than pistols?

Mr. Hair: Oh, you mean down at the bridge? This was a pistol. And sometimes you carried a shotgun. Sometimes a pistol or shotgun. But that was a regular thing down there.

Paul Stillwell: Well, you wouldn't usually have a pistol, though, for hunting.

Mr. Hair: No, no, that's true. No, you would have that for protection. They were mainly for your protection. And a lot of people carried those for their own protection. That's why I say like on the weekends, that's when so many people were getting shot up.

Paul Stillwell: We were talking about your high school and the sports, were you in any other extracurricular activities?

Mr. Hair: In plays and the drama department and stuff like that.

Paul Stillwell: What sorts of plays were you in?

Mr. Hair: Oh, I can remember one that we had there that was really terrific. Find it's so appropriate for the Golden Thirteen here. It was called "The Thirteenth Chair." It was one of these voodoo things where all the lights went out and somebody rose up. It was something to that effect, one of these voodoo mysteries or something.

Paul Stillwell: Like "Friday the Thirteenth."

Mr. Hair: Yes, it was one of those things. It was called "The Thirteenth Chair." It was great; it was good play.

Then, you see, we had what we called one-act plays that were really sponsored by Bethune-Cookman College. They would invite the high schools up during the summer time to put on these one-act plays, and they got awards, whoever put on the best play and stuff like that. So you participated in things like that. We presented one that was called "The Sod," I remember. It was about life in Ireland with the people living in old sod houses and something like that. And things of that nature.

Paul Stillwell: How much awareness did you have of the Navy while you were growing up?

Mr. Hair: You mean in elementary school and whatnot?

Paul Stillwell: Well, in junior high and high school and college. Was that something that the black community was aware of?

Mr. Hair: Oh, yes, yes. Definitely so. We were aware of the Navy. I guess I became aware of it around high school time.

Paul Stillwell: What sort of perceptions did you have of it?

Mr. Hair: Well, at that time I mainly saw it as a part of the military, one branch of the military service: the Navy, the Army. They were the main two branches. I guess that was about it at that time.

Paul Stillwell: Was it something that interested you at all as far as wanting to go into?

Mr. Hair: Not through high school, no. After I got into college and the war started and all of that, that's when I started leaning toward the Navy as the branch of service that I wanted to go into.

Paul Stillwell: When you knew you'd have to go into something?

Mr. Hair: Yes, that's right, because of the war situation. And I wanted to go into the Navy because I always loved the water. Plus I did not like the color of the army uniforms.

Paul Stillwell: You told me about that one before.

Mr. Hair: Yes. Yes.

Paul Stillwell: How much means did you have of learning about or keeping up with black culture? Did you, for example, subscribe to black publications?

Mr. Hair: See, when I worked in the drugstore there, we had several black publications. And the one thing that the people looked forward to getting were two of our leading black newspapers. They were the *Pittsburgh Courier* and the *Chicago Defender*. And every week we had them there, and they sold well, considering that time and that community there. They sold very well. So you always looked forward to that. Plus occasionally we'd put on different programs about different aspects of black life and whatnot. Some of the churches would sponsor different things. So it was on a limited basis, but we had some of that. And the school always took quite an interesting part in that sort of thing.

Paul Stillwell: Have *Ebony* and *Jet* taken the place of those two newspapers you mentioned as far as today's situation?

Mr. Hair: Well, I don't think they've taken the place of those newspapers. I think that so many other black publications have come out that you don't have the great need for those papers now, because it's being taken care from a local level. For example, here in this city now we've got about, well, we've got the first daily black newspaper going now. It's just beginning. It's called The *Challenge*.

But on a weekly basis we have *Amsterdam News*, which is old now, we have *The City Sun*, and then in Long Island here, we got *The New York Voice*, the local paper for Long Island. Therefore, because of that, at least around here, we don't get those other papers anymore now, like the *Pittsburgh Courier*. The other one comes from Chicago, you know, and they went out throughout the whole country. Now you've got a lot of these local papers.

Paul Stillwell: Well, I was thinking on terms of *Ebony* and *Jet* as magazines intended for a national market.

Mr. Hair: Yes, right. Oh, I see what you mean. So in that sense, they have. Yes, definitely.

Paul Stillwell: What are you initial memories of enlistment and first getting involved with the Navy?

Mr. Hair: Oh, well, initially, well, that started in New Orleans because I was there, because I had an educational deferment for one year.

Just before my graduation I got my announcement again from the Army that I had to report, and about July 1, 1942. Right away then I knew I wanted to go in the Navy and that's when I started exploring around with the Navy about the possibilities of going in.

Well, when I went to the recruiting center there in New Orleans, that's when I was greeted and all. Of course, there was a lot of competition there between the Army and Navy. I knew all about it back then. The recruiting person there talked with me about it, and I told him if I had to go in I wanted to go into the Navy and so forth. He encouraged me to come in. But at the same time, he was telling me about the Navy and what a wonderful branch of service, and then he patted me on my back and he said, "Look, come on in here. Come on in and sign up, my little French boy." Well, he was giving me a message then to go in as something other than black. And so, anyway, I told him I had to think about it. I would be back. I was trying to handle it kind of diplomatically. But I knew that I was finished with that, so I left there.

After that, I left there and I went to Florida because I had a few more days before my time was up going to report to the Army. That's when in Jacksonville I met Chief Alexander, this black recruiter under the new Navy program that they had started to recruit blacks. They brought in blacks from the teaching profession, physical education schools, and whatnot, to be recruiters. They changed their program altogether. I talked with Alexander about it, and he told me about how they were changing the enlistment policy. Now I could go in as this able-bodied seaman and go into any branch that I wished to. And he could swear me in right there. So with that, I said, "Well, that's fine." Then I told him, "Well, I've got to go back to Fort Pierce to get my clothes and things, and I'll be back tomorrow."

He said, "Fine." So I came back the next day and about 50 other guys came along with me, and we were all sworn in there at the same time and took off for Great Lakes.

Paul Stillwell: Well, I've got a hypothetical question. What if the two choices had been to go into the Army or to go into the Navy in the steward's branch. Which do you think you would have taken?

Mr. Hair: That's a tough question. That's a tough question. I doubt that I would have gone into the Navy, even though I liked it very much. I think I would have gone into the Army—probably opted for something else, Air Force or whatever. Get into Tuskegee someplace, but I don't think I would have gone into the Navy, although I loved the Navy very much. But I don't think so.

Mr. James E. Hair, Interview #2 (11/10/88) – Page 180

Paul Stillwell: Well, it's fortunate then that that opportunity came when it did.

Mr. Hair: Yes, that's right.

In fact, that's why I was scouting around at first to find out what the thing was, see. And this guy was telling me to go in as French. Because I know I questioned him about it.

Paul Stillwell: So you must have gotten in right after it opened up.

Mr. Hair: I did, I did. In fact, it was news to me when Alexander told me about it, when he assured me of the other. That's why I say I was really impressed with him. I thought he was a very honest man and so forth. I accepted his word for it, although I hadn't seen it written there. But he told me I could, so I accepted his word for it.

Paul Stillwell: What do you remember about getting your uniforms and all the check-in procedures at boot camp?

Mr. Hair: That was something. When we got there, of course, they had this huge drill hall, and everybody had to go through this physical. We went to that, and not only the physical but then you also had to go to a psychiatrist or psychologist; I think it was a psychiatrist. He would ask you a few questions. He only asked me two or three like, "What's your name? Where are you from? How much education do you have?"

I told him what degree I had and he said, "Go ahead."

Paul Stillwell: You don't exactly need a psychiatrist to ask those questions.

Mr. Hair: Yes. Know what I mean?

But after I told him about my schooling, he said, "Oh, go ahead." He winced. He said, "Oh, my God, this man coming into this branch of service here with that kind of degree? Oh, my." I guess that was more or less the reaction I got from people. And he winced at it and said, "Oh, go right ahead." And that was it. And then the physical, and then you lined up and they gave you your clothes and all that sort of stuff. And then back to your barracks for your boot training.

Paul Stillwell: How well did you adapt to the navy-type discipline?

Mr. Hair: I didn't have any trouble with the discipline, except, I guess the thing that I had the most trouble with was in the morning eating those hard beans on a piece of toast. That was really difficult. That was really different.

I don't mean to say it was easy at all getting into that line of discipline, because at times it was very rough. If everything went along as planned, it would be fine. But in those days, you see, we slept in hammocks. We had this bay, and I guess about eight or ten of us in each bay. We had this schedule we had to be up at 0500 or something like that every morning. You go out and drill and then to breakfast and so forth. And I had trouble eating those beans on a piece of bread. They were cold by the time you got back to your seat. That was difficult for me to take.

The other thing that was really tough was when you get there at night, and by that time you were dead tired already from all this boot training all day long, drilling and running and calisthenics and all this stuff. And then to have, say, like 2:30 or 3:00 in the morning, the officer of the day would come by and find a little piece of paper under one of the beds that some guy had decided to get a Baby Ruth bar or something to eat at night in his hammock and drop the paper on the floor. Well, then they turned the lights on and said, "Get up." And here we had to go out and drill.

Well, everybody was just about, "Boy, if we could just find out who that guy is, we'd kill him." That was rough, but that was a part of it, and we finally adapted to it. Then I was in good physical shape, anyway, so I could take that.

Paul Stillwell: Well, I've heard that part of the rationale for that is that if you're out on board ship, you may have to wake up in the middle of the night and defend your ship, so you had to get used to doing that. Maybe the officer threw the paper down.

Mr. Hair: Yes, that's right. But you had to work together as a team, because you had to defend that ship. So you couldn't do it all by yourself; you had to depend on every guy on board that ship. Just like you ring general alarms, it's everybody. It's no one individual. So that was the whole concept of it, which was great. But, as I say, it was difficult in the beginning getting accustomed to that, but once you got into it, then you would accept it. Of course, we let the guy know who dropped that paper down, he'd better not drop it again.

Paul Stillwell: They'd find some other excuse to . . .

Mr. Hair: Yes, no doubt about it.

Paul Stillwell: Did you have a chance for liberty while you were in boot camp?

Mr. Hair: Yes.

Paul Stillwell: What sorts of things did you do on liberty?

Mr. Hair: We'd go to Chicago, and in those days the first thing I'd do is look for the YMCA. Usually that's where I stayed, at the Y. And then from there you would find out about different programs that they were giving. Sometimes the Y would have programs; somebody else would have programs. They had a USO there, too. Now, that was terrific. They put on a lot of entertainment: singing and other forms of entertainment there. That was really great. Because you had a lot of people coming out to help to entertain us, the servicemen. So that was really great then.

Paul Stillwell: Did you make contact with the black community in Chicago?

Mr. Hair: That was in the black community.

Paul Stillwell: Oh, I see.

Mr. Hair: See, this was on the South Side of Chicago there, where we went.

Paul Stillwell: Jesse Arbor's old stomping ground.

Mr. Hair: Yes. Because they had a Y out there also, and it was predominantly black. And, in fact, I'll never forget there that when I stopped there, this was the first time I ever came in contact with, I guess it was marijuana or something. But they caught me by surprise, because we were all there in this place in the Y, or maybe it was at the USO. Anyway, it was a place where they provided rooms there for us to stay and they had cots where we could sleep. There was a group of us around there, and we were all talking, servicemen. I was in the group, but I wasn't aware of what was going on until the guy next to me said to me, "There's a roach down there." No? And right away I thought literally he'd seen a roach or something. But this was my first time hearing about it. I looked around and said, "I don't see him."

He said, "Oh, no. It's on my shoe." And there was this cigarette he had on his shoe. But it must have been marijuana or something like that.

But I told him, "No, no thank you. I don't want that." That was my first time coming in contact with that sort of thing. I knew it had to be that because I knew he was high. I could see he was high.

Paul Stillwell: One generally doesn't think of it being used in that era.

Mr. Hair: That's right. That's why I was surprised. I don't know whether it was marijuana; I didn't know what it was.

Paul Stillwell: I think you're right. I've heard that term.

Mr. Hair: Yes, but he called it a roach. What was in it I don't know and I wasn't interested in finding out. I knew it was something he had undercover there. I said, "No, I don't need that sort of stuff."

Paul Stillwell: Did you have a chance to get up to Milwaukee at all?

Mr. Hair: Oh, yes. Now, that was a very interesting place. They had a lot of good programs there, although, I really attended very little of them. Because you didn't get out that often on liberty. But I did go up there once or twice.

Paul Stillwell: I've heard that Milwaukee was very hospitable to servicemen.

Mr. Hair: It was, they were. And, because I remember being up there once, and they were telling us once about how Marian Anderson was there for a concert, and through some way or another, she got the first housing development started there for blacks at that time.* It was a very progressive city there. That was the impression I got there in very few times.

Paul Stillwell: Did you ever get invited home for dinner with a family?

Mr. Hair: This was in boot camp, boot training. No, I don't remember getting invited for boot dinner during my boot training. Because, as I say, we didn't have liberty too often.

Paul Stillwell: You certainly got used to inspections, I'm sure, during your time in boot camp.

Mr. Hair: Oh, yes, yes. Oh, yes, many of them.

Paul Stillwell: Personnel, and rifles, and barracks.

Mr. Hair: Oh, yes, yes. No doubt about it.

Paul Stillwell: Did you also have inspections during the officer training?

---

* Marian Anderson was a noted black contralto who had gotten national attention when she sang at the Lincoln Memorial in 1939.

Mr. Hair: No, no, I can't remember inspections. I don't remember any. I guess the biggest emphasis was on hours of study and things of that nature and different things we had to do. But I don't remember any inspections though. We may have had one or two, but I can't recall them right now.

Paul Stillwell: Did you have any position of leadership within the company you were in?

Mr. Hair: Yes. I came out as the honor man for my company.

Paul Stillwell: What did you do to achieve that?

Mr. Hair: I remember at times serving on the color guard and helping out in another place—I think with the mail—and assisting the commander in some other things. I've forgotten now what they were. But they were little details that they would assign you to.

Paul Stillwell: Did you march the group around at all? Give the commands?

Mr. Hair: Mainly at times I would assist the commander, because most of the marching in our company was done by the commander.

Now, it seemed like I can remember at times he may at times tell you to do this or do that with the group. Drill them down and back, or something like that. But he was the one, really, in charge and you just assisted him.

Paul Stillwell: Was that a chief petty officer?

Mr. Hair: Yes. Right, chief petty officer.

Paul Stillwell: Was he a black man or white man?

Mr. Hair: He was white.

Paul Stillwell: Were the instructors in your classes white, also?

Mr. Hair: In the boot camp, in the quartermaster school, and whatnot?

Paul Stillwell: Well, I was thinking more in boot camp.

Mr. Hair: In boot camp they were mostly white. In fact, all of our instructors were white, with the exception of one or two. They were just about all white.

Paul Stillwell: Well, blacks didn't have much chance to get senior enough at that point.

Mr. Hair: No, it wasn't until later on that, I guess after we left there because they started bringing in some black instructors. But ours were all white.

Paul Stillwell: Did you develop any close relationships with your fellow boots? Develop any buddies?

Mr. Hair: Oh, yes, yes. There were many out there that were really great. In fact, I remember there was one guy out there from Chicago. His name was Gamble. He and I got to be very close there, buddies and whatnot. And several others. But you lose contact with them after a while. Of course, the one guy that was close to me, A. T. Smith, was holding my high school ring for me, and I never saw him after that. The guy went out one night, and that was it. So I've never heard from A. T. since then.

Paul Stillwell: And you've had to live your life without that.

Mr. Hair: Yes, that's right. Yes, indeed.

Paul Stillwell: What differences do you recall then when you got into the quartermaster training? Probably it was a more relaxed type situation.

Mr. Hair: It definitely was. It was definitely much more relaxed and was a lot of schoolwork, a lot of training there in the quartermaster school, which included the signal school also. We had a combination of them then. But it was a lot of work that we had to do, a lot of studies. We had to attend a lot of classes. Some were visual classes like sighting and recognizing all of our military planes, and things of that nature. None of the enemies, just ours.

Paul Stillwell: That's curious.

Mr. Hair: Yes, yes. It is understandable, though because, see, at that time the principle behind it was that if we knew each one of our planes, any other plane that showed up there right away you'd know it was the enemy.

I remember they used to use the principle of the counterfeit money. And real money, you see real money all your life. Now but all of a sudden you see something different. But I'm saying this course was more intensive then, you see, that would be. They use that as a sort of illustration.

It was really good, though. We had an old chief there running that thing. And imagine you're going on all day and then after this, we'd drill and then a lot of the guys were tired, especially if it was hot because they started in the summertime.

Some of the guys had a tendency to snooze off. And right at that time he had all of these planes up there showing them on the screen, he would stick in a nude picture of a girl. Well, that would cause a reaction and would wake those other guys up. Then these guys missed everything. "Oh, man, you missed it."

But they were terrific classes. Now, along the same line, I never will forget in gunnery class there. We went through all these different schools, and this guy was showing us how to break down a gun and reassemble it. And to do it within a certain amount of time and so forth. And so this instructor—I'll never forget him—he came up and he said, "Look here, boys, I'm here to teach you gunnery. I'm only doing it because they told me to. I know you don't need it, because when you get out there in the Pacific to fight those stupid Japanese, you won't need a gun. They're so stupid, all you need, boys, is just a hammer, and hit them over the head."

So I said, "You're not going to see me out there with just a hammer."

Paul Stillwell: Especially against those airplanes.

Mr. Hair: Yes, that's right. But it was a terrific program.

Paul Stillwell: Did you get into navigation and piloting?

Mr. Hair: Yeah.

Paul Stillwell: Celestial navigation?

Mr. Hair: We got into some of that there. We got into some of it—not too much celestial navigation then. It was more or less dead reckoning and things of that nature. We did have some celestial navigation but not much.

Paul Stillwell: Well, you probably felt right at home with the piloting.

Mr. Hair: Oh, yeah, yeah. That wasn't difficult at all, the dead reckoning and all that. You know, the old measuring line that we had—deep six and so forth. I've forgotten the scale. Fathom and whatnot.

Paul Stillwell: The lead line.

Mr. Hair: Yeah, the lead line, yeah. Fathom was, what, the first six feet up, something like that?

Paul Stillwell: Six feet up.

Mr. Hair: Yeah. But that was, that was all great.

Paul Stillwell: So were you rated then as a third class when you finished that up?

Mr. Hair: Yeah. Third class, yeah. Third class quartermaster.

Paul Stillwell: What do you remember of your specific duties on board the *Penobscot*?

Mr. Hair: Aboard there I was given the duty of being quartermaster, and I was to keep all of the charts updated. I had to make all the necessary amendments on those charts, like shipwrecks or new buoys, or new fixes, everything, which we got every week from the Coast and Geodetic Survey, something like that. And so you had to keep all those things up to date, plus to keep the skipper then abreast of any of these changes.

So, basically, that was it. And, of course, you kept a daily log on every day of everything. What did we have to do? Have to enter that thing every 15 minutes or something like that.

Paul Stillwell: Well, really, I think it went more by events, a course change, or speed change, or sighting another ship.

Mr. Hair: Yes, yes. That's right, it did. When you were active, you had something going on all the time, so you'd fill that book up in a little while.

Paul Stillwell: Did you get involved in taking bearings and plotting them?

Mr. Hair: Not in the tugboat. Not then, and the reason for it was because we didn't need much of that data, see, because we were mainly around the New York area, and we didn't go much below the New Jersey shore. In other words, we didn't get out of sight of, say, the Ambrose light, or some big fix that we knew there. So we just said we sighted this and so forth. But all the buoys and things around, and markers all around New York and this area around here, I was well aware of all those things. You had to keep up with those things every day. Not only that, but the time element, flashing every two seconds, five seconds, ten seconds, whatever it is, whether you know what light that is.

Paul Stillwell: How well did the crew get along together in that type boat?

Mr. Hair: I must say that they got along very well there, and it was an integrated crew there. This was when the Navy first started integrating. But it was a good group. First of all, in that time we had an old skipper there that his main thing was all he wanted was a good beer. But in addition to that, we had a boatswain there who was very outgoing and just seemed to know how to get along with people. It was the personality of the men who really made that thing go. And because of that, everybody just seemed to develop a wonderful relationship; they were very friendly, very outgoing toward one another. And I can't remember any incident there where we had any trouble at all. And, as I say, the skipper there, too, was a wonderful guy. Of course, he did his job and he was able to relate to the crew there very well. So all that really helped quite a bit.

Paul Stillwell: Was the skipper a commissioned officer?

Mr. Hair: Yes, right.

Paul Stillwell: Like a lieutenant junior grade?

Mr. Hair: No, in the beginning he was a chief warrant officer.

Paul Stillwell: I see.

Mr. Hair: Yes, chief warrant officer. Right. Which in those days was a commissioned officer.

Paul Stillwell: Did you feel a sense that you had to prove yourself when you got on board?

Mr. Hair: Oh, yes. Yes, I did.

Paul Stillwell: How long did it take before you felt like you were accepted?

Mr. Hair: I'd say six weeks to a couple months before that came around.

Paul Stillwell: There was some skepticism initially, I guess.

Mr. Hair: Yes, right, right. It was. Because here I was moving into, shall we say, a position that we had not really been in before. Although at that time we had a few other blacks on there that were like coxswains, which helped out a lot.

Paul Stillwell: Right.

Mr. Hair: And so that really helped a lot. But it took quite some time. After that, then they seemed to accept me all right.

Paul Stillwell: Did you have seamen working for you when you were a quartermaster?

Mr. Hair: Oh, yes, yes.

Paul Stillwell: How did they react to you?

Mr. Hair: In the beginning it was very cold, very cold. As I say, it took a while before they would accept. Quite a while.

Paul Stillwell: And that may be true for anybody, white or black.

Mr. Hair: Right.

Paul Stillwell: The new guy has to show that he can do the job.

Mr. Hair: Yes, no doubt about it. Because it was the same thing when I became skipper. They're going to wait to see what you can do. And then once you do it, boy, then they come to feel very confident about you. "Oh, I'll go to sleep." One of those sorts of things. But it does take time on those things.

Paul Stillwell: Are there any really highlight experiences from that time on the *Penobscot* that you remember? Any specific incidents?

Mr. Hair: The thing that I remember so much about that *Penobscot* out there was that this was an old steam reciprocating engine in that thing. We were out there laying a steel net, not alongside but sort of to an angle of Ambrose Channel. It was a fence to prevent any enemy submarines from coming in there. So we were working on that and, say, about 200 feet back here from those steel nets is where we had to work in there with these magnetic mines that they had laid.

Paul Stillwell: That got your attention, didn't it?

Mr. Hair: Oh, yes, indeed. So we had to be most careful not to hit one of those darn mines there.

In those days you had the old bell system. One bell—I've forgotten now the terms we used for it—one bell so much speed ahead; one bell and a jingle, full speed ahead; and then two bells quickly means reverse from that your first stop. One bell, first stop. See, I mean all these things. Now, down in that engine room was all this noise. The guy running the engine down there couldn't always hear these bells. Oh, we had a lot of close calls out there. [Unclear section]

We had several of those events out there. It was really rough out there. That was the most dangerous job. In fact, when I came back as skipper of the tug, one of the first assignments, to go out there to help repair those nets again. That was something else, because you really had to be careful out there. Fortunately, I didn't have that old steam reciprocating engine because that thing was rough. It was a powerful thing, but we had a

13-foot screw on there. But imagine that thing would hit a mine out there; we'd have long blown to pieces.

Paul Stillwell: Well, on the subject of *Penobscot*, quartermasters traditionally steered the ship quite a bit. Did you get that experience?

Mr. Hair: Oh, yes, very much so.

Paul Stillwell: Probably pretty good at it from what you'd done before.

Mr. Hair: In fact, that was very helpful to me when I became skipper, because I'd had a lot of training on handling ships and whatnot. Because we did docking at times, and assisting in docking and things of that nature, plus all kinds of towing and whatnot. So it was really something.

I never will forget the day we had a job in assisting in the towing of a big dry dock from Bayonne, New Jersey. It was a huge thing that was taken out to the Pacific someplace or someplace.

Paul Stillwell: Floating dry dock.

Mr. Hair: Floating dry dock. Now, towing that thing was really something.

But it was all from that kind of experience that really helped me to later on decide what I did when I was a kid.

Paul Stillwell: That's a heavy dose of seamanship.

Mr. Hair: Oh, yes. No doubt about it.

Mr. Hair: And I think you mentioned before that you'd been involved in working with the battleship *South Dakota* after she'd come back from the Pacific.

Mr. Hair: One time we did assist a little bit, right.

Paul Stillwell: What's involved in working with a big ship like that?

Mr. Hair: Well, usually aboard ship like that you had a pilot aboard. And then from his position aboard the ship, he would give you a signal, which was usually a whistle. You'd get his straight path ahead of time, which was going to be your signal. Two short toots, and then he'd give you the signal what he wanted—come ahead or where to push or where to back off.

So you took your position, which might be toward the front bow of the ship where at a certain point he might want you to push that ship into the dock or just hold it up there against the tide or something. But the pilot gave you the signal on those things.

Paul Stillwell: It's easier now. They have walkie-talkies to do that.

Mr. Hair: Oh, yes. Right.

Yes, in those days you could really get fouled up, because you couldn't hear all the time. The guy was way up there on the battleship someplace, and you were way down here trying to hear, a lot of mixed signals at time in those things. There were not too many, but occasionally you'd get a missed signal.

Paul Stillwell: Especially you were talking about the problem down in the engine room as well where it was very noisy.

Mr. Hair: That's right. And some days especially if you got high winds or something or stuff like that, you couldn't hear the guy if you were on the other side.

Paul Stillwell: What were the crew accommodations like in the *Penobscot*?

Mr. Hair: You mean in terms of their sleeping arrangements and all that?

Paul Stillwell: Eating, and laundry, and all that.

Mr. Hair: We had all of that aboard ship. Sleeping quarters, we had these little, like bunk beds that would fit against the bulkhead. In daytime they were turned up. Nighttime you'd let them down a little. The mattress was in there, and you'd sleep there. But you get used to that sort of thing, especially on those icy cold days. You just touched that bulkhead, and it was really cold, really cold. You got used to those things.

The eating and all that were very good, particularly if you had a good cook. Now, if you didn't have a good cook, you would be overdrawn in a little while.* You had to watch your stores. When I was skipper aboard the old yard tug, we were fortunate that we got this cook who used to cook for an admiral, and the reason why we got him, he was too old to go to sea. But all those things were very well taken care of and, fortunately, we had good cooks except one time we had a lousy cook aboard the *Penobscot*. And the chaplain was bawling him out every day. But other than that, everything was fine.

Paul Stillwell: I know that when you were going through the officer training then back at Great Lakes, you had the professional subjects. Did you also get training in how to be leaders? Was that part of the curriculum?

Mr. Hair: I guess that was throughout the curriculum, you might say, because we always had it drilled in us, even with Goodwin there, that to be an officer, you've got to walk this way, and do this, and carry this step this way. In other words, you can't be a leader unless you demonstrate this in this way. So I guess that was always a part. But in terms of a course on that, I don't remember that specifically.

Paul Stillwell: Anything else about that officer training period that we haven't covered? That's really the essence of what these interviews are about. That's what drew you all together.

---

* Navy ships are allotted a certain amount of money per crew member per day for food. To be overdrawn is to have spent more than the amount allowed.

Mr. Hair: Yes.

Paul Stillwell: Were the classes mostly lecture-type or solving problems, or how would you describe that?

Mr. Hair: They were mostly lecture-type classes, and, as I say, we had to do the work. As I mentioned earlier, some of the officers doing the teaching there were really not interested in our learning. But they'd throw it out to you, "Now, here it is. If you can do it, do it." It was one of those type things.

So in that sense we had to do a lot of the work ourselves. But I think, as I told you before, it was interesting from the group point of view, though, in going to school that I believe, in reading the histories of the others, we all more or less concur that, certainly the majority of us, didn't know that we were selected for this Officer Candidate School.*

Paul Stillwell: Well, you didn't know initially, but you found out pretty quickly.

Mr. Hair: Yes, we found out soon. But some people were saying, "Oh, you must have known about this a month or two in advance." No, no, that wasn't it.

Anyway, when we first got together, it was my first time meeting the other members of the group, possibly with the exception of Lear. Though Lear was not in the same company, I could see Lear at Great Lakes. It was one of those things, although I didn't know him personally. So we got there and met, and I came from the Third Naval District, Nelson came from another naval district, as I recall. But then the other guys, I believe, all the other guys came from either Hampton or Great Lakes. Some of them knew each other before I got there, and so I guess it might have been the same as Nelson where we really didn't know the group until we got there. So that was my first really meeting the group then.

---

* After the first round of interviews with members of the Golden Thirteen, each man then received the transcripts from all the others.

Paul Stillwell: What were your initial impressions? Did you find them a likable bunch?

Mr. Hair: [Laughter] No, when I got there, I thought them as a bunch of guys who were very curious about, "Gee, what's going to happen here?" and this sort of thing.

Paul Stillwell: That's understandable.

Mr. Hair: Yes. And then Commander Armstrong told us about what this was. I'm sure some of them knew what it was then, but no one was saying anything, more or less, until it was official, as I recall.

But at that time I really had no idea about them per se because I guess we were all caught up into what was going to happen to us now. Everybody was really wondering about that aspect of it.

Paul Stillwell: Then you grew closer together as you experienced this thing together.

Mr. Hair: Oh, yes, yes. Once we got there as a group, then we really started growing very close together. And we knew we were in there together. I guess it goes back to the old concept of the Navy that you're a group and you've got to work together, and we recognized that. We really got together right from the beginning.

Paul Stillwell: When did you personally find out that you were going to be commissioned?

Mr. Hair: Well, it was toward the end of the school, maybe a day or two. I know it wasn't very long that they called us in and, as I recall, they sort of called in each one individually. At that time they told us that we were then going to be commissioned officer in the Navy, the first officers. Somebody made that announcement. And who in the heck was it? I can't remember. But that was about the first time I knew about it.

Paul Stillwell: Who gave you the oath?

Mr. Hair: I don't remember. I don't remember.

Paul Stillwell: Again, it was individually, I take it.

Mr. Hair: As I recall, it was more or less of a group thing, I believe, where they just said that you are now officers, or something to that effect.

Paul Stillwell: The others I've talked to seem to remember that it was an individual type thing. Then there was a coming together to take these various pictures.

Mr. Hair: Yes, right. Oh, yes, that's right. There was. I guess it was an individual thing, but I can't remember who the person was that gave it to me. I don't remember. If they said that, I'm pretty sure that was right then.

Paul Stillwell: The Navy has really made you much more heroes in retrospect than it did at the time.

Mr. Hair: Oh, yes, yes.

Paul Stillwell: It was really a low-key thing.

Mr. Hair: Oh, yes, no doubt about it.

Paul Stillwell: Except for that *Life* magazine coverage.

Mr. Hair: Yes, right. That was about it. That was about it.

Paul Stillwell: What do you remember about going to get your first officer's uniform?

Mr. Hair: Well, I went over to Finchley's in Chicago. I'm sure it was Finchley's where they sent us. Somewhere we got this place we inquired about where we should go, and

I'm pretty sure it was Finchley's. I think we had a certain amount of money they'd given us to buy uniforms. We went over there and Reagan had gone over there, and I guess so many fellows went with me, and we bought these uniforms. And that was it. I don't remember anything unusual about it. We just got our uniforms and came on back.

Paul Stillwell: What kind of reactions did you get when you started wearing the uniform out in public?

Mr. Hair: Oh, that was something. Everybody stood up to look. Some crossed the street so they wouldn't have to salute you, and all that sort of stuff went on. It was a terrific thing. Some people were just outright stunned by it, it looked like, amazed that this had happened. I can remember some saying, "Oh, gee, what should I do now? Should I salute or what?" Then you had the others that followed right along with the proper protocol and saluted and so forth. But you had every kind of reaction imaginable there.

Paul Stillwell: Well, you probably didn't get any absolute out-and-out disrespect, did you? They couldn't be that bold, could they?

Mr. Hair: Well, no, except, as I said, there were some who would cross the street rather than speak to you or anything like that than salute you, or things of that nature that you would have. But there was nothing outright. Only thing is it was clear to us that we had certain limitations in terms of the officers' club and where we could go, and things of that nature. That was still pretty clear.

Paul Stillwell: How did you feel about that?

Mr. Hair: Well, it didn't surprise me at all at the time, put it that way. It didn't surprise me. I knew it wasn't right, but yet at the same time, I wasn't expecting them to open up the officers' club to us, unfortunately, at that time because of the situation. I really didn't.

Mr. James E. Hair, Interview #2 (11/10/88) – Page 200

Paul Stillwell: Well, and you lived with that situation for a long time.

Mr. Hair: That too. That's right. I knew that to just change overnight, I didn't hold those expectations up. It was just one of those unfortunate things.

Paul Stillwell: What kinds of feelings of pride and satisfaction did you have at that point?

Mr. Hair: Oh, I felt a great deal of pride in the fact knowing that through the help of so many others, I finally made it to become a naval officer. It was a great thing; it was a wonderful thing. As I said before, I accepted with the spirit of thanks to the people who made it possible, because I couldn't have done it on my own.

Paul Stillwell: And it wasn't the sort of goal that you could aspire toward, because it didn't exist before you came along.

Mr. Hair: Yes. That is so true. Absolutely.

Paul Stillwell: How long did you stay around Great Lakes before you went out to your tug?

Mr. Hair: Not very long. And the reason for that was very simple because, you see, I was still attached to the Third Naval District. And I don't know whether Dennis Nelson had the same sort of orders. See, I was just like loaned to this program except I had to go to this school from the Third Naval District, and I had to return to the Third Naval District. So it was only a matter of days, as I recall, that I was there. Maybe a week, maybe five days or something like that. I got orders to come back, you know, to Third Naval District. This was when I came back and reported to Captain [Unclear] over here in Tompkinsville and the Third Naval District here.* That's when he assigned me as skipper aboard the *YTB-215*.

---

* Tompkinsville is a neighborhood in the northeast part of the New York City borough of Staten Island.

No questions asked, he just assigned me to be skipper. I was over here, and he had done his homework. Captain [Unclear] was no stupid guy. He wasn't going to send you out there if you didn't know anything.

Paul Stillwell: What were the satisfactions of being in command of your own boat?

Mr. Hair: Oh, it's a great satisfaction there. I guess one of the biggest satisfactions was knowing that you could be skipper of a boat on which the crew really respected you. And they really, really admired me, in a sense.

Paul Stillwell: How soon did that sense develop?

Mr. Hair: It was some time after that, but it wasn't as long as, say, going aboard the *Penobscot* as quartermaster. I guess the reason for that was because I had worked in the Third Naval District before and some of the people that knew me or knew of me—one of those sorts of things. They knew I'd been steering the tug around before that.

Because of that, I'd say it didn't take many weeks before they began to accept me. And, of course, I guess the big thing came when, I think, one of my first assignments was out there between the nets and those mines. When you maneuver and work in that place without going to pieces, pretty soon the guys are going to respect you. Nothing more than saved our lives.

But they became very comfortable with it. It was an integrated crew, and in that situation it really didn't matter whether they were black or white. They all looked at you in the same way, "Can you do the job?" It was one of those things.

Paul Stillwell: That was a difference from Sublett and Martin going out to the West Coast, because there they took the white sailors off and replaced them with black crewmen.

Mr. Hair: Yes, yes. Right. No, they didn't do that here in the Third Naval District. We had a great group of guys there. I was really fortunate, though, that when I first went aboard I had this boatswain's mate around who used to work on Swedish sailing vessels. He could literally run up a mast pole like a monkey. So when you've got that kind of person as a teacher, that helps with all these other guys. They look up at that guy, and they say, "Boy, this means I got to do this too?" This is what it takes. So it was things like that that served as a great thing, and then, as I say, I got this elderly fellow who didn't want on battleships anymore that used to be the cook for admirals and he was some outstanding guy, outstanding cook. We were always falling underdrawn on what came up out of stores, and he was an outstanding cook.

But all these things really add something. Then we started having shows aboard the ship whenever we got a chance to because most times you were working day and night on these things. One of the interesting things about this cook we had was that he must have been at least 65 years of age. I don't know how he happened to stay in the Navy. But a young guy at heart. His name was Blake. During the show time one of the biggest parts of the entertainment, he would get up and tap-dance. He must have been about 300 pounds. Not a big fat guy, just a big man. He could tap-dance, and sing a little bit, and all this sort of stuff. It was a show just put on right by the group. So all this thing got big applause, and before you know, you had a terrific group there together. I'm telling you, it was really terrific.

Paul Stillwell: That builds togetherness too.

Mr. Hair: Yes. It really did; it really did.

Paul Stillwell: Well, one of the satisfactions of command is that you're the ultimate boss.

Mr. Hair: Yes, yes. No doubt about that.

Paul Stillwell: And, of course, it's also a burden too. You've got nobody to pass the buck to.

Mr. Hair: Yes, along with being the boss is a great responsibility, see. You've got to always be aware of the fact that you have a responsibility to your men there. And, as I said, the great success is because I couldn't be that boss—in an effective way—unless I really had their approval in a way. Once I demonstrated to them that I really knew how to handle this ship and I could carry out the orders, and so forth and so on, they functioned. I think I had only one guy that that came up on a captain's mast or something like that.[*]

Paul Stillwell: In our first interview you mentioned the guy that didn't replace the light.

Mr. Hair: Yes. Actually he forgot about it. But you don't accept forgots, and they knew it in the service. And I let him know we can't accept forgots. No, you've got to carry out your responsibility first. And that really stood up well with the entire crew, even the guy himself. He didn't resent it after that. I made him steel-wool polish buckets and things of that nature. But that was about the extent of it.

Paul Stillwell: Did you put an emphasis on keeping the boat shipshape and looking smart?

Mr. Hair: Oh, that was always there, yes. Absolutely. Let me think about that. That's something that I did not have to pound them about. They just did it, and it was always in shipshape with the exception of that time that guy didn't put that light bulb up there. But other than that, it was one of the neat—even Captain Meyer spoke about how neat that ship was.[†]

Paul Stillwell: I think that's one of the reasons that he was so impressed by you.

---

[*] Captain's mast is a sort of court in which the commanding officer of a unit listens to requests, awards non-judicial punishment, or issues commendations. Most often captain's mast is used for punishment of lesser offenses than those that merit courts-martial

[†] This is a reference to the skipper of the destroyer escort *Mason*, in which Hair later served under Lieutenant Commander Norman Meyer.

Mr. Hair: Yes, that's right. It really was; it really was. Beautiful fenders on the sides that were all handmade there by the crew.* Paint jobs throughout. It was really, really something. And that engine always ticking just right.

Paul Stillwell: Did you have mixed feelings in going from there to the *Mason*?

Mr. Hair: Oh, I did, yes. Right, right. Because, on the one hand, I was very glad and very elated because it was really a promotion to go aboard the *Mason*. The *Mason* was an outstanding ship. It was *the* black ship at that time.

Paul Stillwell: And also a warship.

Mr. Hair: A warship, man-of-war, that's right. And to be sent to the first black ship built there, that was quite an achievement. So I was really glad in that sense. But, on the other hand, my mixed feeling was I hated to leave this wonderful tug and this wonderful crew that I knew so well. When I left there, a lot of those guys were in tears.

Paul Stillwell: Of course, you were giving up command, as well.

Mr. Hair: Yes, that's right. That's right. No doubt about it. Giving up the command, but at the same time, it was a promotion.

Paul Stillwell: Well, you really sketched your duties previously pretty briefly on board the *Mason*. If you could discuss those in more detail, please.

Mr. Hair: Well, actually, I went aboard there as a first lieutenant, meaning that I was in charge of all deck operations. And this is basically what my duties covered there at that time, was to keep all deck engines and things in full operation, all the boats, and all those sorts of things that we had aboard there. To keep them in working condition, to see that

---

* A fender in this case is a device put over the side of a ship or boat to absorb shock when she makes contact with a pier or another ship. It is particularly useful in the case of a tugboat that routinely pushes up against the sides of ships.

the ship was always in shipshape condition, make sure that it was neat, clean, and in good order at all times. Basically, those were my duties aboard ship there at that time.

Paul Stillwell: Did damage control fall under you also?

Mr. Hair: Yes, it did because I remember I'd gone to damage control school out in Philadelphia. I remember that. I went down there a week or so for that. So I had that, shoring and all that sort of stuff.

Paul Stillwell: Firefighting?

Mr. Hair: Yes. That was all a part of it, right. Firefighting and all that went into it.

Paul Stillwell: So you were a department head in that ship?

Mr. Hair: Yes.

Paul Stillwell: What do you remember about watch standing?

Mr. Hair: You know, I remember once we were up in Maine, and I had the watch then at nighttime. That was about the main time there when we had to arrange for all kinds of shore patrols and things of that nature, and go out in certain areas and patrol. See that your men stayed in proper line and so forth. But on a few occasions I did watch standing.

Paul Stillwell: Did you stand watches under way?

Mr. Hair: I don't recall standing watches under way. No, I don't recall that, no. I don't recall that; I don't recall.

Paul Stillwell: Describe what Captain Meyer was like when you had the meeting with him. What was he like to serve with as a skipper?

Mr. Hair: He, as a skipper, he was always concerned about his ship, the condition of his ship and also the crew. How his crew was doing, how they were functioning, and how they were getting along, and so forth. He always came across to me in the sense of being a military person who was very much in charge, and very much concerned about his crew and his ship.

Paul Stillwell: He strikes me as the kind of officer who would set very high standards, both for himself and for the ship.

Mr. Hair: Well, he does, no doubt about it. He does set very high standards. But, at the same time, he's very realistic. I found him to be very realistic. I remember having stopped in Bermuda and places where, even during the years of war, he had certain ideas about protection of his ship, and so forth. And he'd take this all in consideration in terms of who would get liberty and things of that nature. His ship and his crew came first, but in those areas he was quite realistic about the job.

Paul Stillwell: Was there a sense of letdown when that ship went out of commission?

Mr. Hair: Oh, yes, no doubt about it. In fact, everybody there really felt very down when they said that that ship was—it was like you're leaving home. Now you're no longer going to have the ship, and, I guess, for the best of all of us they did it in a very quick way in that we were there, as I recall, no more than about a day, and we got our orders where we were going after that. We just left the ship there for the decommissioning.[*] Because, yes, they picked all the officers and the crew there, but most of us, anyway. The captain stayed there with it then, you know, but the rest of us depleted, you know.

But there was quite a letdown on that to see your ship be decommissioned. In fact, I was down there this past summer in Carolina, and I wanted to go out there just to see if that old USS *Mason* was still out there. I imagine it's no longer there now.

---

[*] The *Mason* was decommissioned at Charleston on 12 October 1945.

Paul Stillwell: Probably been scrapped.*

Mr. Hair: Yes, probably so.

Paul Stillwell: Was there a special feeling about the *Mason* on the part of the crew that we are the Negro ship?

Mr. Hair: Oh, yes, yes. No doubt about it; no doubt about it. I don't think that that was just there aboard the *Mason*, but I think that happened before about the people who knew about it, because they always looked at that with a lot of pride it gives a man-of-war to carry a black crew. It really gave them a lot of pride and feeling that way. I know I did even before going aboard there. I used to look forward to the day when I would just see the *Mason* coming into New York Harbor. Every week you just had ships coming in, and you just hoped you see it one day. So people really had a lot of pride in that ship, the ones who knew about it.

Paul Stillwell: Did the ship get any special publicity because of the crew?

Mr. Hair: I'm sure it did in the beginning, but I wasn't there in the beginning of it, because, initially, they had another captain on there.

But I'm not aware of what that publicity was. I don't know how we heard about it. I mean we in terms of the people over in Tompkinsville. But we knew about the *Mason*. I've forgotten now how we got the news about it, in the papers or what. I guess we'd gotten to know about it through schools, and whatnot, the Navy was planning this ship and it had an all-black crew. Jesse talked about it and some of the others, so we knew about it in that sense. So we really looked forward to it. But, specifically, coming to the publicity, I really don't know.

Paul Stillwell: Did you have any contact with the *PC-1264* either while you were in the

---

* On 18 March 1947 the former USS *Mason* was delivered to Thomas Harris for scrapping.

YTB or the *Mason*?*

Mr. Hair: Yes.

Paul Stillwell: When? What sort of contact?

Mr. Hair: Well, the *PC-1264* was another ship that we looked up to at that time because it meant that we got more blacks that were able to move up in terms of man-of-war ships. The *PC-1264* was one of those. They docked there in Tompkinsville right near where we used to dock. So on occasion, I would go around to that pier just to take a look at it, *PC-1264*. And occasionally I would talk to some of the crew there and ask them questions about the ship: "Oh, man, how is it? How does she take to sea?"—seaman questions like that. And they all really were very responsive to that. They were really, honestly, very proud of that *PC-1264*. I knew what they'd been in because they had some trouble with the engine. They had to replace the engine or something like that, like with any ship coming out brand new sometime. They did a lot of experimentation with them, you know. So they were laid up over there for a while over that. Not in Staten Island, but they were around.

But, anyway, I did get to speak to some of the fellows aboard ship there, and they thought very highly—the response I got from them was a very positive one.

Paul Stillwell: This is when you were still in the tugboat?

Mr. Hair: When I was an enlisted man, and also right after I became an officer. So I saw them both times.

Paul Stillwell: Well, any more recollections you had with the *Mason*?

---

* The submarine chaser *PC-1264* was the other warship with an all-black enlisted crew in World War II. Her first black officer, Ensign Samuel L. Gravely Jr., reported aboard in the spring of 1945. He subsequently became the U.S. Navy's first black admiral.

Mr. Hair: I think I related the others to you that we had there on the *Mason*. I can't think of any others right now. I can say this, though. I remember one of the criticisms; I heard it one time that the *Mason*'s crew was not up to par, or something like that. I don't remember what the reasons were.

Paul Stillwell: Well, that was Justice White's perception that commanding officers, if they had to send some of their people away, would not send the best people.

Mr. Hair: Yes, right. Right. Yes, right.

But throughout the Navy I found that on different ships some people there that were more qualified than others. And I think this was appropriate to the *Mason* at that time. But as far as the crew is concerned and their dedication and all that, it was terrific. I can recall one ship there in Staten Island, the captain couldn't take off with that ship because the crew hadn't shown up yet. That's right. We had some of those things. Especially during the time when the Navy had the policy whereby if a captain had a misfit aboard his ship, he could just transfer him off. Eventually a bunch of these misfits ended up on one ship. Now, that is what I found about when I saw that ship there in Tompkinsville where the captain couldn't take off. Pretty sure that's what he had, was a bunch of misfits. But, fortunately, the *Mason* didn't have this problem. These were a bunch of dedicated guys and when you said, "0400 we're shoving off and everybody better be back at 0200." They were there. It was that sort of thing.

So in that sense it was great, but just like any ship's crew during the war then, you had to keep training even when they were aboard ship a lot of times, because you never reached the point where you knew it all. You had to keep going in that direction. So in that sense, I thought the *Mason* did an admirable job.

Paul Stillwell: Then all of a sudden she was decommissioned, and all that went away.

Mr. Hair: Yes, that's right. That's right. And I'm still trying to locate some of the guys who were on there.

I think I told you about a fellow I met in Philadelphia was telling me that he knew one of the guys that was aboard there. His father's a rabbi here in New York. And I still haven't gotten over to that synagogue yet, but I hope to get over there one day to see if I can locate the guy.

Paul Stillwell: Well, then you went on board the LST. Do you have any additional recollections to record about her?

Mr. Hair: Let's see, *LST-1026* was in China. Never forget that. That was a great experience out there also.

I think I mentioned to you most of those wherein we were transporting Chiang Kai-shek's armies. We served from Haiphong, Indochina at that time up to Manchuria. That was quite something because every day we had to drop so many overboard. Or, rather, they did. They always did because they were basically very weak, and a lot of them had dysentery or whatnot. So it was very bad. But there I was in charge of all ammunition and stuff aboard ship at that time. We had a skipper there from Wyoming. I'm sorry I can't remember his name. He was quite a guy, and gray, all Navy, that sort of thing. He was there to carry out his job, and he did a terrific job.

Then we transported troops up to Manchuria and some up to Chefoo, China, up there on the Gulf of Pohai. So it was many of those things. They gave us that big party, and we all started fighting one another up there because they were giving out all these things. I think I told you they gave me 40 bottles of 40-year-old brandy. And mine was just a minor gift. Imagine what the captains got. Oh, my goodness, it was really something. But that was about it. And then—here we go again—the *LST-1026* was decommissioned in the Philippines. After that I got my orders to head home, got them in Subic Bay.

Paul Stillwell: Then you got on with the rest of your life.

Mr. Hair: Yes. I told you before the interview about the tender that we took to Pascagoula, Mississippi.

Paul Stillwell: Well, that was earlier, though, when you were still enlisted.

Mr. Hair: Right, right, right.

Paul Stillwell: Well, you didn't tell on tape the sequel, about this thing that you got in the mail from Pascagoula.

Mr. Hair: Oh, yes. I guess one of the other things I should bring out here in all my experiences here, there were two ships that I was on in which I was the only black aboard there. One was this torpedo tender, which we just took down to Mississippi. And the other one was the *LST-1026*. So those were the only two ships that I served on where I was the only black aboard ship.

And there I didn't encounter any trouble once I got aboard the ship. Before I got aboard the ship there was a lot of trouble.

Paul Stillwell: You're talking about going to China on the troop transport.

Mr. Hair: Right, right, right, see.
So that was about the highlights of that, though.

Paul Stillwell: Did you feel a sense of elation in getting out of the Navy and getting on with your planned career?

Oh, yes, but there again it brought some mixed feelings. I was very much elated that the war was over and that now I was getting out and I was going home to pursue my career. I was looking forward to that. I was going home, and, of course, I had contacted my folks that I was coming to see them in Florida, soon going to be a big homecoming there. But only to get there to find that my brother had just been run out of town. So I said, "Well, here we go again." It was one of those things, and it was a rough homecoming; it was a rough homecoming.

Mr. James E. Hair, Interview #2 (11/10/88) – Page 212

But we finally worked that through somehow or other and made it. But it was no elation. It was no joyful celebration or anything. It was back to the grind again, so to speak. And it was a very, very disappointing experience.

Paul Stillwell: But still you wanted to get on with that civilian career rather than stay in the Navy.

Mr. Hair: Oh, yes, yes. No doubt about it. I did. Although I loved the Navy, I didn't want to stay in. I wanted to get out then, because I was looking forward to following my career, going back to school, and then, hopefully, getting married and having a family, and so forth, things of that nature.

Paul Stillwell: And you probably had no idea, either, what opportunities would be available in the Navy.

Mr. Hair: Yes, that's right. I knew it was going to be rough because, you see, we couldn't just stay in the Navy. Couldn't just stay in the Navy.

Paul Stillwell: Well, how did Nelson stay in then?

Mr. Hair: Well, Nelson fought it, see. Nelson was a real fighter, real fighter. Now I wasn't up to it at that time to really fight the situation. Because after then I tried several times to even get into active units of the reserve, which you had to be in in order to keep it alive. And that was difficult; that was very difficult. I talked with several people about it, and whatnot.

Paul Stillwell: Did you do it?

Mr. Hair: I tried several times, like I went and inquired down at 90 Church Street and different places around, different units, and so forth. So finally I found a fellow in school with me, named Oprey, and he told me he would be able to get me in his unit over in Brooklyn in the navy yard there.

So I said, "Okay," then with this sort of pull—something that you really needed then—some kind of contact to get it. I said, "Okay, I think I will." But, anyway, something or other, something just kept telling me, "No, no, don't do it; don't do it." And I didn't get in. He made a date with me to meet with this captain to discuss it, and so forth. Anyway, I didn't do it. And then the next thing I knew, after I didn't join, why, the next week the unit was sent out to Korea, see. But Oprey didn't have to go because he had a disability.

So I saw him after that. I said, "What are you trying to do, get me back into the war again?" But that was different. But Nelson fought it, you see, Nelson was a fighter.

Paul Stillwell: Well, John Reagan was called back on active duty.[*] Was any kind of approach made to you like that?

Mr. Hair: No.

Paul Stillwell: And Gravely was too.[†] They were looking for blacks to help with recruiting.

Mr. Hair: Yes, right, right. This was a few years after that.

Paul Stillwell: It was about '49, somewhere in there.

Mr. Hair: Yes, '49, '50, right. I used to receive mail from the Navy regularly all during that time. But I didn't get anything on that. Not that I recall.

---

[*] John Reagan of the Golden Thirteen was called back on active duty to serve as a recruiter and stayed in for a while.
[†] Lieutenant (junior grade) Samuel L. Gravely, USNR. The Korean War started while he was on recruiting, and he eventually remained on active duty until his retirement as a vice admiral in 1980. See Gravely's Naval Institute oral history.

But, as I say, the main thing was that I had served in the Navy, and I just didn't want to stay in at that time. No. But I did make some attempt to stay in the Navy Reserve in some of the active units.

Paul Stillwell: Well, we covered your civilian experiences. We discussed, also, the reunion on board the *Kidd* in 1982. Are there any highlights you want to talk about from the other reunions with the Golden Thirteen?

Mr. Hair: I guess the one that comes to mind right away is the one out in Great Lakes, Illinois, where they dedicated the building to the Golden Thirteen. I think that was a most memorable occasion out there. Certainly one that I'll never forget. I think it was just a terrific thing on the part of the Navy, the Navy command and all who made that possible. And it shows a great sensitivity for the Navy. And, not only that, but I think it really helps—I know I use this a lot when I go around to the schools—to show what the Navy has done now in terms of blacks. I use that as one illustration.

Paul Stillwell: How much do you do in terms of public appearances and recruiting?

Mr. Hair: Most of the public appearances are during Black History Month. But occasionally other things will come up. For example, I was over at Clark College in Atlanta, Georgia. It was having an affair and I was invited there. They would introduce me as one of the first black officers in the Navy, ask for a few remarks, and things of that nature. And we talk about the Navy, different opportunities and things. Those sorts of things happen, but infrequently between the other times.

Then, like Admiral Miller invites me over for his graduation over here, New York Maritime College, and things of that kind.[*] I got an invite from Rhode Island up there. Of course, I didn't make that one. I couldn't get up there at that time.

---

[*] Rear Admiral Floyd H. Miller, USN (Ret.), served as president of the State University of New York Maritime College from 1982 to 1995 after leaving the Navy.

And, and a few other cases—a paper in Florida there that I know in Fort Pierce, the *Chronicle*, a black newspaper that has quite a good circulation, just did another article on the Navy and James Hair, one of those sorts of things. So there's quite a bit of that.

That brings up a very interesting point that I put in my letter to the Golden Thirteen just recently, because Sylvester brought up a very interesting thing. Because we were challenged down there at the convention to go out and recruit one candidate for officer. Syl brought this up in his letter, saying he was still trying to do this. Would we give him advice on how he could do this, some tips or something. In my response to him, I was saying that, "You know, Syl, I agree with you and I wish I could do it, too, in a hands-on fashion to say that, 'Here is Lieutenant Joe Cook I really recruited for the Navy,' personal, hands-on sort of thing. But I haven't been able to do that yet where I can just say, 'This is the guy.' But I know there are guys in the Navy now who have gone in as a result of the Golden Thirteen, but not through me personally." But my point in bringing this out is that when I listen to unsolicited speeches, like by General Petersen from the Marine Corps—black guy—Admiral Toney in the Navy, Admiral Hacker from the Navy, where they stood up before us in unsolicited speeches and talked about how much we meant to them because the Navy made us black officers in the Navy, and how it motivated them.[*]

I was saying, "It would be my guess that this has worked many, many times, but personally I don't know the people. I think it's there, and I think this is the thing we've got to continue to do, to recruit in this way even though we don't do it hands-on." That was just my idea that I gave to Sylvester, you know. My letter went to all of them. I shared it with all of them, my thoughts on it.

Paul Stillwell: Well, just by what you've accomplished, you can serve as a source of inspiration.

Mr. Hair: Right, right. I think it was a great experience and a great opportunity that we had there too.

---

[*] Lieutenant General Frank E. Petersen Jr., USMC; Rear Admiral Robert L. Toney, USN; Admiral Benjamin T. Hacker, USN.

Paul Stillwell: Well, we didn't talk much about your family when I was here before, and it's always a great source of pride to a father. Would you like to discuss your children, please?

Mr. Hair: Yes, right, surely.

I have three wonderful children, a son and two daughters. And they're all now married; and they're all well, and doing well, and getting along fine. I have seven grandchildren—five grandsons and two granddaughters. I might say that, unfortunately, my wife and I separated and divorced after 35 years, but I understand she's doing all right. But, anyway, the children are all doing very well. And I'd like to say, too, that during the times of our conflict, we never really brought our children into it, fortunately. This is one thing that we agreed on, although this does affect children. I don't care what age they are. Of course, when they're young, it's more. But, fortunately, all of ours are grown and married. My son is with an insurance company.

Paul Stillwell: What's his name?

Mr. Hair: Jimmy. He's a junior, James Jr.

Paul Stillwell: How old is he?

Mr. Hair: He born 1952. He would be now, what, 34, 35, 36 coming up, something like that. And then I've got a daughter two years older than he is, Danita. And then I've got a younger daughter that's two years younger than my son.

Paul Stillwell: What's her name?

Mr. Hair: Janette Susan, but we always called her Susan. My first daughter's name is Margaret Danita, but we always called her Danita. That was a carryover from family background. We usually did that with the girls. And, as I said, my son works with an of years. And, interestingly enough, Lieutenant Phillips, who was the exec on the *Mason* when I went on there was working with insurance of North America, which is the company that my son joined up with later on. But not in Philadelphia; here in New York. Yes, right, here in New York. Of course, he's with another company now.

He and his wife—my daughter-in-law, Wanda—they have two sons. I have two grandsons there. There's one that's James III. The other one is Brandon Lee. Then my oldest daughter is married to a lawyer who is with First Boston, corporation lawyer, and they have three children—twin boys, identical twins, and a granddaughter. Then my younger daughter, they have a boy and a girl, see. They are the youngest of the girls just now, a year to the boys, three and a half now. They are housewives. In fact, that's the school that my daughter's children attend.

Paul Stillwell: The New Canaan Country School.

Mr. Hair: Right. Look at that constitution, would you?

Paul Stillwell: Looks about like my son's handwriting.

Mr. Hair: Isn't that great, though? Isn't that great that they got that idea there? That's really great. Look at that.

So, thank God, they're all doing well. Getting along all right. All is going well with them, so I've got a lot to be thankful for.

Paul Stillwell: Well, I'm thankful for the opportunity to get to meet and know you, Mr. Hair. It's a genuine pleasure.

Mr. Hair: Yes, yes, same here.

And I might say, too, this is not a precedent or anything, but I'm really proud of the fact that all my kids went to college, finished college, and whatnot. It's really something.

Paul Stillwell: You've got a lot of blessings to count.

Mr. Hair: Oh, yes, I certainly have. And every day I try to count them too.

Paul Stillwell: You mentioned that you wanted to talk about the baseball caps that are lined up on your couch there.

Mr. Hair: No, I just put them there for you to see them. But they remind me to tell you the story about the USS *Lake Champlain*. The one that I related to you earlier, before the recording started.

Paul Stillwell: I'd like to hear that one.

Mr. Hair: I was telling you about it when I got the invitation to go to the commissioning.

Paul Stillwell: Well, we didn't put that story on tape, though.

Mr. Hair: Well, anyway, after I'd come back from my conference in Atlanta, Georgia, and vacation this summer, I came home to find this letter here. It said Department of the Navy, Pascagoula, Mississippi, and here in big bold letters, it says, "U.S. Official Mail." And it said, "James E. Hair." When I saw this, my first thoughts went back to the day when, as a quartermaster, we took this new torpedo tender down at Pascagoula, Mississippi. And that's the first thing that came in my mind. My reaction was, "Oh, what the hell is this? I know damn well we delivered that ship to Pascagoula, Mississippi." I thought maybe they were inquiring of us, "What did you do with that ship?"

But, anyway, to my surprise, I opened it up and there was this wonderful invitation to attend the commissioning of the USS *Lake Champlain* here in New York

City, which was docked right opposite the USS *Intrepid*.* But the USS *Lake Champlain* was built in Pascagoula, Mississippi, and, hence, the invitation from there.†

But it took me some time before I could calm down as to wondering what the heck this was all about.

But it was a wonderful experience. I'm sure there are many other things that could be added to it, but, unfortunately—it's really difficult to remember everything that happened 40-some years ago.

Paul Stillwell: I can understand that.

Mr. Hair: And this is one of the things that Norman Meyer, the former captain of the USS *Mason*, and I were going through with, trying to recall those things. And it's very difficult.

Paul Stillwell: Well, I much appreciate your effort and you have recalled a great deal.

Mr. Hair: Oh, thanks a lot.

Paul Stillwell: Thank you for that.

Mr. Hair: I'm just grateful for the opportunity and I know a lot of the stuff I've done is sort of in a disjointed way but I don't think the future historians would worry too much about that, as long as they can get the story out.

Paul Stillwell: That's exactly right.

Mr. Hair: I think this is a great thing about our Navy, and the future of our Navy, and what this is going to mean, and for our country. And I think it's a wonderful thing, and

---

* The last of the ASW carriers, the *Intrepid* (CVS-11), was decommissioned on 15 March 1974. In 1982 the ship opened as a museum berthed at Pier 86 on the west side of Manhattan.
† The *Ticonderoga*-class guided missile cruiser *Lake Champlain* (CG-57) was commissioned on 12 August 1988, a few months before this interview.

I'm darn proud that I could be a part of it. And, again, with thanks to so many people who made it possible.

Paul Stillwell: Thank you again.

Mr. Hair: Yes. Thanks very much, sir.

Launched in 1969, the U.S. Naval Institute's award-winning oral history program is among the oldest in the country. Used in combination with documentary sources, oral histories offer a richer understanding of naval history through candid recollections and explanations rarely entered into contemporary records. In addition, they help depict the atmosphere of a particular event or era in a manner not available in official documents.

The nonprofit Naval Institute accomplishes its history projects solely through contributed funds and gratefully accepts tax-deductible gifts of all sizes for this purpose. This support allows the Institute to preserve the life experiences of today's service men and women so they may enlighten and inspire future generations.

For information about opportunities to underwrite Naval Institute oral history projects, please contact the Naval Institute Foundation at 291 Wood Road, Annapolis, Maryland 21402; by phone at (410) 295-1054; or by e-mail at foundation@usni.org.

Index to the Oral History of
Mr. James E. Hair

Alves, A.
Black petty officer who went through officer training with the Golden Thirteen at Great Lakes in 1944 but was not commissioned, 53-54

Arbor, Jesse W.
Enlisted sailor who became one of the Navy's first black officers in 1944, 62-63, 116, 122, 144, 147

Armstrong, Captain Daniel W., USNR (USNA, 1915)
Officer in charge of training black sailors at Great Lakes, Illinois, during World War II, 41-43, 52-56, 58, 70-71, 75, 117, 143-145

Barnes, Phillip G.
Enlisted sailor who became one of the Navy's first black officers in 1944, 59, 65-66, 124-125

Barnes, Samuel E.
Enlisted sailor who became one of the Navy's first black officers in 1944, 59, 66-67, 124, 129

Basketball
Hair played on segregated teams in the 1930s, 9-11, 171-174

Baugh, Dalton L.
Enlisted sailor who became one of the Navy's first black officers in 1944, 69, 112, 117, 144, 147

Bethune, Mary McLeod
Black educator who was president of Bethune-Cookman College in the 1930s, 23-24, 31, 37, 113, 131-134, 156-159, 169-170

Bethune-Cookman College, Daytona Beach, Florida
Hair attended the school in the late 1930s after graduating from high school, 23-26, 131-134, 152, 156-157, 169-170, 176

Charleston, South Carolina, Naval Base
Two black officers had dinner at the officers' club without incident in late 1945, 88-89

Chiang Kai-shek
As President of Nationalist China shortly after World War II, 95

China
    The U.S. tank landing ship *LST-1026* transported Chinese troops and relief supplies in the Far East in 1946, 95-98, 210
    In Shanghai in 1946 American naval personnel had to be wary, 96-97

Communist Party
    Concern about in the United States, 1930s-50s, 151-152

Cooper, George C.
    Enlisted sailor who became one of the Navy's first black officers in 1944, 59, 66-67, 78-79, 125-126, 146-147

Dille, Lieutenant John F., Jr., USNR
    Served on the staff of the Great Lakes Naval Training Station in 1944 during the training of the first black officers, 57-58, 140-142

Drugs
    In 1942, while he was on liberty, Hair was offered marijuana, 183

Enlisted Personnel
    In 1943 on board the Navy tugboat *Penobscot* (YT-42), 45-50, 189-190
    In 1944-45 on board the Navy tugboat *YTB-215*, 201-204
    In 1945 on board the destroyer escort *Mason* (DE-529) 207-209

Federal Bureau of Investigation (FBI)
    In 1943 investigated prospective members of the first officer candidate training class for African Americans, 149-151

Florida Agricultural and Mechanical College, Tallahassee
    Hair attended the school briefly in the late 1930s, 27-29

Golden Thirteen
    Training of the first black naval officers at Great Lakes in early 1944, 40-44, 54-79, 116-121, 136-150, 195-200
    Reunions in the 1980s of members of the Golden Thirteen, 109-112, 121, 158-159
    Legacy of the group, 113-115
    Dedication in 1987 at Great Lakes, Illinois, of a building named in honor of the Golden Thirteen, 158-159, 214

Goodwin, Reginald E.
    Enlisted sailor who became one of the Navy's first black officers in 1944, 42-44, 70-71, 77, 117, 143-144

Great Lakes, Illinois, Naval Training Station/Center
    In 1942 black sailors received training at Camp Robert Smalls, 39-45, 180-189
    Training of the first black officers in 1944, 40-44, 54-79, 116-121, 136-150, 195-200

Dedication in 1987 of a building named in honor of the Golden Thirteen, 158-159

Hair, James E.
Parents, 1-7, 26-27, 114, 130, 153, 160-162
Siblings, 2, 6, 14, 18-20, 23, 28, 129-130, 159-161, 211
Wife, 50, 101
Children, 102, 216-217
Grandchildren, 102, 216-217
Temporary alternate spelling of his last name as H-A-R-E, 136-139
Growing-up years in the 1910s-30s in South Carolina and Florida, 1-21, 131-139, 153-155, 161-178
Athletic endeavors in high school and college included basketball, 9-11, 171-174
Work and college in the late 1930s-early 1940s, 22-36, 131-134, 152-153, 169, 176
Enlistment and training in the Navy in 1942, 39-41, 178-189
Service in 1943 on board the Navy tugboat *Penobscot* (YT-42), 45-54, 189-195
Went through officer training at Great Lakes in early 1944, 40-44, 54-79, 116-121, 136-150, 195-200
Commanded the Navy tugboat *YTB-215* in the New York City area in 1944-45, 17, 79-84, 90-91, 118-119, 200-204
Served in 1945 on board the destroyer escort *Mason* (DE-529), 75-76, 84-88, 91-92, 204-209
In 1946 was first lieutenant on board the tank landing ship *LST-1026*, 95-100, 210
Postgraduate education circa 1950, 76
Civilian career in social work, 101-110
Reunions in the 1980s with other members of the Golden Thirteen, 109-112, 158-159

Hong Kong, British Crown Colony
Liberty site for U.S. naval personnel in 1946, 98-99

***Kidd*, USS (DDG-993)**
Site of a 1982 reunion of surviving members of the Golden Thirteen, 109-112

***Lake Champlain*, USS (CG-57)**
Commissioned at New York City in August 1988, 219

Lear, Charles B.
Enlisted sailor who became one of the Navy's first black officers in 1944, 40-41, 72-73, 121-124, 149, 196

Leave and Liberty
For black sailors in Chicago and Milwaukee in 1942, 182-184
For black personnel in New York City during World War II, 50-52, 90-91, 155-156
In Shanghai, China, in 1946 American naval personnel had to be wary, 96-97
In Hong Kong in 1946, 98-99

Life Magazine
    In April 1944, published a photo of the first black naval officers and subsequent letters to the editor, 128-130

Louis, Joseph (Barrow)
    Famous boxer whom Hair met in New York City during World War II, 155-157

LST-1026, USS
    Carried Chinese troops and relief supplies in the Far East in 1946, 95-100, 210
    Decommissioned in the Philippines, 100

Martin, Graham E.
    Enlisted sailor who became one of the Navy's first black officers in 1944, 73-74, 77, 120-121, 127, 144

Mason, USS (DE-529)
    Destroyer escort that was commissioned in World War II with a crew of black enlisted men, 75-76, 84-88, 91-92, 204-209

McIntosh, Ensign John, USNR
    In 1945 became the second black officer to serve in the destroyer escort _Mason_ (DE-529), 88-89

Meyer, Lieutenant Commander Norman H., USN (USNA, 1935)
    In 1945 commanded the destroyer escort _Mason_ (DE-529), which had a black enlisted crew, 84-88, 91, 203, 206

Mine Warfare
    The Navy had a defensive minefield near New York City in World War II, 46-48

Naval Reserve, U.S.
    After World War II, Hair was unable to make a connection to stay in the reserve, 212-214

Nelson, Lieutenant Commander Dennis D. II, USN (Ret.)
    Enlisted sailor who became one of the Navy's first black officers in 1944, 53, 67, 74-75, 77, 117-118, 196, 212-213

News Media
    In April 1944, _Life_ magazine published a photo of the first black naval officers and subsequent letters to the editor, 128-130
    Article in _The New York Times_ in April 1982 about a reunion of the Golden 13 on board the guided missile destroyer _Kidd_ (DDG-993), 109-110
    Newspapers published in the 1920s-30s for black readership, 177-178

New York City, New York
    In 1943 the Navy tugboat *Penobscot* (YT-42) operated out of the port of New York, 45-52, 189-195
    The Navy had a defensive minefield near the city in World War II, 46-48
    Liberty in the city for black Navy personnel in World War II, 50-52, 90-91, 155-156
    Navy tugboat *YTB-215* operated out of New York City in 1944-45, 79-84, 90-91, 118-119, 200-204

Payton, Chief Petty Officer Noble F., USNR
    Hampton Institute instructor who in 1944 was involved in the training of the Golden Thirteen at Great Lakes, Illinois, 142

PC-1264, **USS**
    Subchaser that operated in World War II with a black enlisted crew, 207-208

Penobscot, **USS (YT-42)**
    Navy tugboat that operated out of New York City in 1943, 45-52, 189-195

Pinkney, J. B.
    Black Navy enlisted man who went through training with the Golden Thirteen in 1944 but was not commissioned as an officer, 60-61

Propulsion Plants
    Reciprocating steam engine on board the Navy tugboat *Penobscot* (YT-42) in 1943, 192-193

Racial Issues
    Segregation in Florida and Alabama in the 1920s and 1930s, 5-6, 11-23, 37-38, 165-174
    Lynching of Hair's brother-in-law Estes Wright in Florida in 1935, followed by unpleasant aftermath, 14-23, 37-38, 78-79
    Skin bleaching and hair straightening products for black citizens in the 1930s and 1940s, 171
    The Navy opened general service ratings to black sailors in June 1942, 38-39, 178-180
    Segregated training for black sailors at Great Lakes, Illinois, during World War II, 39-45, 54-79, 116-121, 136-150, 180-189, 195-200
    In 1944 a white pharmacist's mate used a stick to whack the penis of a black officer candidate at Great Lakes, 64-65
    Two black officers had dinner at the Charleston officers' club without incident in late 1945, 88-89
    Hair had unpleasant experiences on board troopships while going to the Far East in 1946, 92-94
    Achievements of Presidents Harry Truman and Lyndon Johnson in fostering opportunities for black citizens, 108-109
    Hair's views on affirmative action for minorities, 107-108

Reunion of the Golden Thirteen on board the guided missile destroyer *Kidd* (DDG-993) in 1982, 109-112

Reagan, John W.
Enlisted sailor who became one of the Navy's first black officers in 1944, 75-76, 118
Served with Hair on board the yard tugboat *YTB-215* out of New York City in 1944-45, 118-119, 147

Recruit Training
In 1942 black sailors received recruit training at Camp Robert Smalls, Great Lakes, Illinois, 39-41, 180-186

Religion
In Hair's family in the 1910s-30s in South Carolina and Florida, 1-2, 6-7, 14

Richmond, Lieutenant (junior grade) Paul D., USNR (USNA, 1942)
Reserve officer who supervised the curriculum for the training of the Golden Thirteen at Great Lakes, Illinois, in early 1944, 57

Shanghai, China
American naval personnel ashore in 1946 had to be wary, 96-97

Sublett, Frank E.
Enlisted sailor who became one of the Navy's first black officers in 1944, 73-74, 76-77, 136

Training
In 1942 black sailors received training at Camp Robert Smalls, Great Lakes, Illinois, 39-45, 180-189
Training of the first black naval officers at Great Lakes in early 1944, 40-44, 54-79, 116-121, 136-150, 195-200

White, William Sylvester
Enlisted sailor who became one of the Navy's first black officers in 1944, 61-62, 67, 77, 114, 116, 215

Williams, Lewis R.
Black Navy enlisted man who went through training with the Golden Thirteen in 1944 but was not commissioned as an officer, 61-62, 151

Xavier University, New Orleans, Louisiana
Hair attended the school in the late 1930s-early 1940s, graduated in 1942, 30-35

***YTB-215*, USS**
Navy tugboat that operated out of New York City in 1944-45, 79-84, 90-91, 118-119, 200-203

www.ingramcontent.com/pod-product-compliance
Lightning Source LLC
Chambersburg PA
CBHW080614170426
43209CB00007B/1426